Unintended Consequences

Unintended Consequences

Lessons Learned
An Educational Journey

Joe Franks

Herb Appenzeller

CAROLINA ACADEMIC PRESS

Durham, North Carolina

Library of Congress Cataloging-in-Publication Data

Franks, Joe.
Unintended consequences: lessons learned : an educational journey / Joe Franks and Herb Appenzeller.
  pages cm
Includes bibliographical references and index.
ISBN 978-1-61163-128-9 (alk. paper)
1. Education--United States. 2. Teachers--United States. 3. Edu-
cation--Aims and objectives--United States. 4. Educational
change--United States. I. Appenzeller, Herb. II. Title.

LA217.2.F68 2013
370.973--dc23

                                2013004296

CAROLINA ACADEMIC PRESS
700 Kent Street
Durham, North Carolina 27701
Telephone (919) 489-7486
Fax (919) 493-5668
www.cap-press.com

Dedication

I am eternally grateful to my parents for their inspiration and support, and to my wife Tiffany without whom I would not be the man I am today. Her love, motivation and encouragement have enabled me to grow in ways I never thought possible.

—Joe Franks

Walter Lippman may have said it best: "Teachers are the custodians of values."

To: … My son Tom and my daughters, Linda Partee and Mary Somers, and my daughter-in-law, Heather Stanley Johnson, who continue to make a difference in the lives of their students.

… Jane Forbes Roscoe and Clara Jo Macon Pleasants, my outstanding student teachers at Guilford College who inspired countless students during their tenure in teaching.

—Herb Appenzeller

Contents

Preface

Unintended Consequences: Lessons Learned, An Educational Journey is different because it was designed that way. The two authors have a diverse background in teaching over a period of 86 years. Their educational experiences began at the 8th grade and covers 35 years in high school, five years at a private church-affiliated junior college, 37 years at a private senior college, and nine years at three state universities in graduate school where students sought terminal degrees. Both authors agree that there is a common thread of characteristics of the students at all levels of their 86 years of teaching and many years of extra-curricular activities that include coaching sports and administration of sport-related activities. With these highly diverse backgrounds with both common and, at times, unique experiences at various levels, the authors wanted to write about their educational experiences from the 1940s to today. Both authors share personal stories, anecdotes from their on-the-job experiences. Both agree with Thomas Peters and Nancy Austin who wrote in their best seller *A Passion for Excellence*:

> Stories, as nothing else reveal what is important to an institution. Stories convey the mistakes and successes of the past so that others can profit from them.

Bob Gingher, a book editor for the *Greensboro News & Record*, wrote:

> No one develops learning tools by rote, but again by examples and stories.

Gingher concludes that "stories" are the indispensable tools of teachers and students, without them there is no such thing as moral imagination (*Managing Sport and Risk Management Strategies*, 2nd edition, 2003). Author Joe Franks, a gifted teacher with 30 years in the public high school classroom, with special duties as a coach and athletic trainer, has a passion for teaching and being a highly respected role model for students, parents, faculty and staff members. He refers to his past experiences to evaluate the status of education in the 21st century. Franks welcomes criticism of his personal views when he makes his feelings known about education today and his advice on ways to make education relevant and exciting for all students. Herb Appenzeller, with a very diverse background starting in the 8th grade of a rural school in North Carolina, observes education on a predominantly collegiate background. He, like fellow author Joe Franks, uses stories and personal experiences in the educational system for 56 years to make his points about improving the status of education in the 21st century. As co-author of *Unintended Consequences: Lessons Learned, An Educational Journey*, this is the 24th book Appenzeller has written and edited on sport law, sport management, and education.

The authors understand that readers of the text will agree and disagree on various subject matters, but critical thinking on the contents and opinions expressed in the book is much more important. By sharing concerns and opinions about ways to improve teaching skills, we can make education exciting and rewarding for our most important resource—our students and their contributions to life in the 21st century.

Joe Franks
Herb Appenzeller

Acknowledgments

I would like to thank Herb Appenzeller, without whom this book would not have been possible. He is an inspiration. To Robert F. Mays, without whom I would have never become an athletic trainer in high school, which set me on my career path. To Fred Hoover, trainer at Clemson University who mentored me in college. To John Lalonde and Jim Aplington, our team physicians at Grimsley for so many years who helped mold me into a successful athletic trainer. To Jeff Smouse, head football coach at Grimsley who encouraged me to coach, to Bob Sawyer, athletic director at Grimsley who allowed me to leave training to pursue coaching. To Phil Weaver and Mac Morris of the North Carolina Coaches Association who gave me the opportunity to get involved on the state and national levels with coaching. To Robin Lincks, a great friend and coach who set up my first date with Tiffany. To Bert Henderson and Bob Mahony at Clemson who helped me serve Clemson. To Catherine Barnhardt, Kemp Dalton and Suzanne Weaver at Grimsley who have helped make the teaching experience wonderful. To Jay Bennett, Dave Reynolds and Bill Leonard, my high school buddies who keep me young. To Pat McKillip, the most understanding mother-in-law anyone could have. To my over 4,500 students over the past 30 years who have given me the opportunity to teach, and to learn from them. And finally to Mark Zuckerburg, who, through Facebook, has allowed me to reconnect with important people in my life once again.

Joe Franks

To: ... Joe Franks, a special colleague, who gave me the opportunity to join him as co-author of *Unintended Consequences: Lessons Learned, An Educational Journey.* His bold but honest observations of his 30 years as a teacher, coach and athletic trainer endeared him to his students who admired him for his outstanding teaching, mentorship and lifelong friendship. Joe Franks is a life-changer and it was rewarding for me to work together on the book.

... Ann Terrill Appenzeller for her valuable input that made a good book even better.

... Bruce Stewart, former Provost at Guilford College, and more recently, the former Headmaster of Sidwell Friends School in Washington, D.C. Bruce introduced us to the outstanding writing of Patrick Bassett, former Chief Executive of the National Association of Independent Schools (NAIS) and his "6 Cs."

In addition, Bruce Stewart shared his vision of Sidwell Friends School's innovative practices in the 21st century. His futuristic ideas have been viewed by educators in the United States and international leaders. His generous and unselfish information on education in the 21st century was valuable for the book. We appreciate his efforts on our behalf.

... Dr. Annie Clement for her intriguing chapter on "The Future of Sport Management" which was published in *Successful Sport Management* (2008). Her predictions, years ago, came true in a spectacular chapter in *Introduction to Sport Management* (Parks and Zanger 1990). Her predictions for the 21st century coincide with our ideas on education in a remarkable way.

... Dr. Colleen McGlone, Professor of Sport Administration at Coastal Carolina University, for much of the material in the chapter on hazing.

... Luke Somers, my grandson, for his technical skills in the completion of the book. He has a bright future.

... Linda Lacy and Keith Sipe, publishers of Carolina Academic Press, for their continued support and encouragement. They have the vision to publish material on the cutting edge of society.

... many of my former teaching colleagues who influenced my ideas and career in education. These colleagues helped me appreciate the words of Thomas Wolfe, who wrote, "a teacher lights many candles that come back later to brighten their life."

... the 50 students at Northern Guilford High School who gave me the insight of 21st century students. I treasure their efforts and help in understanding 21st century students with an outstanding experience in their classes in Sport Marketing. Our future is in good hands because of their vision for the future.

Herb Appenzeller

About the Authors

Joe Franks

Joe Franks is a career educator. He has been at Grimsley High School in Greensboro, North Carolina for 30 years. In those years, he taught United States History, Sociology and Psychology. He received his Bachelor's Degree in Secondary Education from Clemson University in 1983 and his Master's Degree in Social Science, Secondary Education from NC A&T State University in 1992.

He directed the Sports Medicine program at Grimsley for 16 years as a National Athletic Trainers' Association (NATA) certified and NC licensed athletic trainer before he got into coaching. He served as an examiner for the NATA certification exam for many years and was a facilitator for the NATA instructing examiners. He was an assistant football coach for six seasons and coached golf at Grimsley from 1997 to 2013. His men's and women's golf teams won multiple conference and regional championships and both programs were North Carolina state runner-up. He is a Level III Certified Golf Coach by the Spirit of Golf Foundation.

He was named Guilford County PTSA Council High School Teacher of the Year in 1990, Grimsley High Teacher of the Year in 1997–98 and had the school yearbook dedicated to him twice.

As a student athletic trainer at Clemson University, Joe supported football, soccer and wrestling. He was inducted with the 1981 National Championship Football Team into Clemson's Ring of Honor, has served Clemson on the athletic fundraising group's

Board of Directors, been president of the Piedmont Triad Clemson Club and was chosen in 2001 as one of the 25 Most Intriguing Clemson Fans by the *Orange and White*, a Clemson sports publication.

Since 1987, Joe has been an assistant director of the NC Coaches Association, helping that organization with planning and implementing a coaching clinic that is one of the largest in the country. He was appointed to the Board of Directors for the National Organization of Coaches Association Directors in 2012.

He is married to Dr. Tiffany McKillip Franks, President of Averett University in Danville, Virginia, and enjoys his role as the Presidential Spouse of Averett University.

Herb Appenzeller

Dr. Herb Appenzeller has a varied background in sport as a participant, coach, athletic administrator, professor of sport studies, author and lecturer on the local, state and national level. He was a coach, athletics director and endowed professor of sport studies at Guilford College for 37 years. As professor of education, he had the opportunity to work with student teachers and others on current education practices. After retirement, he taught in the graduate sport administration program at The University of North Carolina, Chapel Hill, and later was Executive-in-Residence in the sport administration graduate program at Appalachian State University. He is recognized as a pioneer in the field of sport law and risk management and author or editor of 23 books in the field. He is a member of eight sport Halls of Fame. As a coach, professor and administrator for over 40 years, he brings a unique and practical body of experience to the sport industry. He has been selected for local, state and national honors, the latest being his third President's Award from the Sport and Recreation Law Association (SRLA), unprecedented in the organization. Appenzeller has been the co-editor of the sport law newsletter, *From the Gym to the Jury*, for 23 years.

Unintended Consequences

Chapter 1

Our Educational System Needs Modification

JF:

The public educational system in the United States was once the best in the world. Can we say that today? Are we the envy of those around the world who produce some of the best and brightest on our planet? Are we the envy of some in our own society who once clamored to get in our schools, or do we see an exodus from our public schools? Too many in our society have given up on our public schools—they are increasingly critical and dismissive. I believe with all of my heart that we still produce some of the best and brightest who can compete with anyone globally, but the system is in need of some modifications. We need to do a better job of ensuring that the children in our public schools receive the best education available, in a safe environment with caring educators and administrators who are committed to student success. If we were truly doing that now, we wouldn't have so many families sending their children to private, parochial and charter schools—or choosing to homeschool. In addition, we wouldn't have politicians working on voucher programs to enable this flight from public education. Why is this happening? Because in too many instances, these alternative schools are providing what the public schools are not. Whether that is perception or reality, it really does not matter. I contend it is the reality of our educational system today, and we need to face it and respond to it. I believe that every time a family removes their child from a public school, it is the fault of the way that our schools are run today. So, we can sit around and study the social, educational and political phenomena; we can establish "blue ribbon" commissions to come up with "pie in the sky" ideas; or, we can rationalize why this has occurred until the cows come home. But these strategies are not solutions. The bottom line is that something has to be done, and we had better act now, or forever hold our peace. If we choose to ignore the problems facing public education, our system will go the way of the dinosaur and cease to exist. What we need are educational bureaucrats and politicians who are not afraid to make tough decisions and allow common sense decision-making back into our educational system. What we must have are people who are willing to stand up and not be intimidated by the politically correct in our society. As callous as this may sound, it is my belief that the needs of the many must outweigh the wants of the few. We cannot be everything to everybody with regard to public education. The system in which I worked for 30 years is so splintered with magnet schools, middle colleges, early colleges, charter schools, virtual schools, traditional schools and block schools that it lacks focus, continuity of mission and identity. We have spread resources so thin in a tight economy that teachers are stretched in ways that diminish the effectiveness of what goes on in the classroom.

Unfortunately, we have learned from societal experience that the squeaky wheel gets the grease, and many times a vocal minority dictates policy. If we let the tail wag the dog with regard to educational policy and ignore what is good for the majority, we will seal the fate of failure in our public schools. Now, don't get me wrong—I am not a doom and gloom sort of person. I am a person who is solution-oriented. It does no good to focus on failed policies of the past. We must learn from the past, but we can't live in it. I tell the young men on my golf team that to be successful in the game of golf, you must stay grounded in the present—let go of the shot you just hit, whether good or bad, because there is nothing you can do about it. Concentrate on the shot you have now, evaluate the variables, visualize a positive outcome and let it happen. If my players begin to worry about the future, they lose sight of executing in the present. By the same token, we cannot dwell on the failed educational policies of the past. We must have concrete ideas of what to do and work to make that happen—in the present. This is reminiscent of a quote I learned from a former Wake Forest University professor, Jasper Memory, who stated this at an orientation for freshmen in 1957. "Be a lifter, not a leaner; a producer, not a consumer; a constructive influence, not destructive. Don't worry about the past—it has gone—or the future—it will take care of itself, but be tremendously concerned about the present; for yesterday is only a memory, tomorrow is only a dream, but today, lived well, makes yesterday a fountain of joy and every tomorrow a dream that has come true."

The solution-oriented ideas that Herb and I propose in this text are not necessarily a quick fix. There is no such thing as a quick fix to complex problems—socially, educationally or politically—but I believe our ideas provide a common sense approach to making the system better, more productive and better for our students—and in the long run, better for our society. It is my hope to stimulate thinking and discussion that can hopefully lead to positive outcomes. Will people find fault with our ideas and criticize them? Of course they will, but we will challenge them to be solution-oriented and not just complain that our ideas can't work.

HA:

Poll: Confidence Drops in U.S. Public Schools

Supporting our opinion, a recent poll "found that confidence in U.S. public schools has dropped to the lowest level in nearly four decades" (*News & Record*, June 21, 2012).

In 1973, the Gallup Poll reported that 58 percent of those polled believed in the educational system in the United States. Since then, confidence by the public in polls revealed a steady decline in the public schools. This poll, conducted on June 7–12, 2012, is based on interviews with 1,004 adults who expressed concern with "churches or organized religion, banks and television news" (*News & Record*, June 21, 2012).

Michael O'Hanlon, senior fellow and director of research for foreign policy at the Brookings Institution writes that "even in a dark hour, the future is bright" for the United States. He describes the educational system of the United States as "the best educational system in the world." He notes that "recent studies estimate that the U.S. has more than half of the world's best 100 universities.... To be sure, our educational system needs improvement, but at the more advanced level, we remain at the front." He concludes, "So yes, let's fix America's problems, but in the meantime let's not lose sight of what is right" (*News & Record*, August 21, 2011).

Our Sputnik Moment

James Campbell, a senior communications manager for the Johns Hopkins School of Education, wrote a column on "A Challenge to Reform: What we could do to fix U.S. schools." Campbell wrote on the bad news about the U.S. public schools that have been "battered by a stream of bad news that has challenged the once proud leader in the world by its leading education systems."

In 2010, a comparison of international testing of students in 34 developed countries revealed "a stunning decline in U.S. test scores." In reading and science, the U.S. was in the middle of the pack and near the bottom in math.

Arne Duncan, Secretary of Education, said:

> The hard truth is other countries have passed us by during the past two decades. Americans need to wake up to this educational reality—instead of napping at the wheel while emerging competitors prepare their students for economic hardship (*News & Record*, January 16, 2012).

Duncan cautions our Congressional leaders to put aside partisan politics to answer the "demands of a highly competitive global economy that requires a skilled workforce." Duncan realizes that the presidential debates of 2012 focused our nation's attention on this problem. His recommendations for the politicians are:

- Rewrite the Elementary and Secondary Education Act, which he describes as a punitive act, known as "No Child Left Behind." He believes the Act is a drag on the nation's schools.
- The new law should focus less on using assessments to penalize schools and teachers and more on student growth and achievement.
- Recruit and retain the best teachers. Most studies show that countries that score high on international tests place a higher value on teaching than the United States and attract their top students into the profession.
- Teachers in the United States feel undervalued as opposed to teachers in other countries who attract the best prospects to teach. Teachers in other countries are respected, and their opinions are valued in curriculum matters and school reform.
- In the United States, 50 percent of teachers leave the profession after five years. The United States needs to design an attractive career ladder for teachers to attract and retain the best.

Duncan points out that the income gap between the poor and rich is now greater than ever in the United States. In fact, the only developed countries with larger income gaps are Chile, Mexico and Turkey.

Researchers Richard Murmane (Howard) and Greg Duncan (University of California at Irvine) published a landmark study called *Withering Opportunity* that says:

> The achievement gap between children from high and low income families is 30 percent higher among children born in the last decade than those born 25 years earlier (*News & Record*, Jan. 16, 2012).

The report supported a theory that "the family has more influence on a student's performance than either school or community." It appears that "if you are born poor, the chances are you'll stay poor." The authors of the *Withering Opportunity* study recommends:

1. Improving the learning environment of low-income children during the early years providing high-quality child care.

2. Universal pre-K programs and economic support such as the earned income tax credits.

According to Campbell: "Some have called the recent release of the international test scores our 'Sputnik moment.'" He concludes: "Hopefully we can resolve as we did more than half a century ago, to once again consider what seems impossible."

Chapter 2

For the Teacher: Why Teach?

JF:

When I was in high school, the last thing I would have dreamed was that five years after graduating I would be back at my old school on the other side of the desk. I am the poster child for "Welcome Back Kotter Syndrome"—I loved it and still do after 30 years. But I'll tell you right now that I am spoiled—I admit it. I have been blessed to be in a great school, with mostly supportive administrators over the years. In my career I taught required United States History, a lower level social studies skills class (which I will talk about later) and have been able to build a popular set of classes that are "senior only" electives. My sociology/psychology electives have been maxed out with kids who have chosen to be there. In those classes, I am spoiled that I have good, mature kids who wanted to be in my class. In essence, I have helped create my teaching position. I couldn't imagine doing anything else.

Over the past years, our school has offered teacher cadet classes for students who think they would like to go into teaching, and North Carolina has had a Teaching Fellows Program that provides college scholarships to students who will commit to a number of years in the public schools. These are great ideas, but they would not have appealed to me in high school or early in college, because a career in education was the furthest thing from my mind. Most 18–20-year-old students don't have a clue about what they realistically want to do in the future, so through trial and error, they narrow their choices in college or wait to pursue a degree. I was one of these — but I did know that I wanted to pursue athletic training/sports medicine in college and work with a major college football program. My initial priorities were extracurricular, not academic, and I went through two majors before settling on education. Yet this was not because I had a burning desire to teach. I figured that teaching would provide the vehicle to allow me to be an athletic trainer and continue what I was truly passionate about. What I found, as many do, is that my college choice was a good one, and my major would be too. Clemson University offered me an excellent education, a sound foundation for my career and a passion for athletics. As I became more involved with the education major, I found it enjoyable and stimulating. When I did my student teaching, I loved it. The students, the interaction, the learning that we did together — this was stimulating and exciting. I knew this was a good choice, even if my initial priorities were a little skewed. Working with athletes was still my passion, but as I was reminded by my high school athletic director and long time friend, teaching is what "buttered my bread" and provided income for my family.

HA:

Teaching Is a Tough Job, But Rewards Can Be Great!

Kim Holden, "a *News & Record*, Four Square Community columnist," wrote about her teaching experience for 37 years. She wrote that people envied her because she had three months off in the summer. She went on to describe how she spent her summer preparing her web pages and "creating a Spanish version for parents who can't read English." She listed the problems she faced financially and the time she spent on schoolwork. However, at the end of the shortcomings she endured, she answered the question of why we teach by giving just one example:

Two of my fifth-graders recently visited. Both were His-
panic, from low income families. The odds were slim that
they could accomplish more than a high school diploma
though both had a great deal of academic potential. Yet
each told me that he had received a full scholarship to
Wake Forest University's Pre-Med program. They wanted
me to know I was the one who had inspired them. Actually, all I did was open the door. They were the ones
who walked through and aimed high.

Holden feels that if America is going to turn things around, "we
need to start by attracting the right people to the profession." She
advocated, "We need the top students to become teachers. We need
to provide full scholarships in exchange for a 10-year commitment.
Salaries need to competitive for all teachers, not just those in science and math."

Holden concluded with a sense of pride when she wrote:

I hope those who can teach will dedicate their lives to
it. It's one of the hardest jobs on earth, *but there is no
greater reward than to know you've changed someone's life.*

After more than 50-plus years in the classrooms at all levels except
kindergarten, I find the author Thomas Wolfe's assessment of teaching the best when he wrote, "A teacher lights many candles that
come back later to brighten their lives."

JF:

An Innate Sense of Creativity:
Teachers Are Born!

I soon discovered that I had a knack for teaching, and over the
years I have come to believe that most teachers are born. A teacher's
personality and demeanor make this job into an enjoyable and satisfying career. Of course, I realize that many teachers are developed

through hard work and training, but successful teachers must have that innate sense of creativity and giving that students buy into. You don't have to be the smartest or the greatest tactician to get students to learn; you have to bond with them. You have to love them for who they are, and you have to be confident enough and human enough to let them see that you are not infallible. At the beginning of each year, I told my students that my worst subject in school was—and I wrote this on the board—"speling"—and they all got a laugh. Spelling is still a weakness, but I told them to correct me, keep me on the right path and that I was not too proud to admit I have made a mistake. Young people are perceptive; they can tell when you try to "BS" them—so don't. I also told them that each class has its own unique personality and that in essence we are on an educational journey together—to learn from the book and from each other. Emil Faber was right you know—"Knowledge is Good." And if you don't know who Emil Faber is, you are culturally deprived—go rent *Animal House* on DVD!

HA:

I graduated from Wake Forest College (now University) in January 1948 and learned of an 8th grade teaching position at a rural school in North Carolina. I would teach a variety of subjects in a self-contained classroom that included North Carolina History, Music, Art, Physical Education, Math, Science and English. I would also coach the baseball and basketball teams.

A former classmate of mine was leaving to have a child and wanted to help me as best she could. She wanted to tell me about the boys in her class who she said were intolerable while the girls were wonderful. I remember so well telling her I wanted to go into the classroom not knowing anything about each student. This turned out to be the best thing I did to begin my teaching career.

When I told the class that I knew absolutely nothing about them, the boys came up after class to ask incredulously, "Do you really mean that you don't know anything about us?" They were relieved and excited over the opportunity to start with a clean slate! At the end of the year, the class, both boys and girls, asked our principal to move me up with them to the 9th grade as their homeroom teacher. Our relationship was strong and rewarding and got my teaching career off to a great start.

One of the important things that led to a successful year may have been the following:

> On my very first day of teaching I saw a group of ten boys going to the Home Economics Building. I recognized them as the basketball players. I asked where they were going, and they said: "We have a game tonight so we are going to rest all day instead of going to class or being on our feet." I told the entire team that I was their new coach, and we would all go to class on game days and never again spend game day in the Home Economics Building. The boys' basketball team had an overall record of 2–13 at the time. We played the top team in the conference that night and upset them. After that a snowstorm that led to 10 days off gave me the opportunity to coach them and install a defense and offense. We then won 12 or 13 games and the Conference Championship. Undoubtedly this made a tremendous difference with my 8th grade students.

We Need More Great Teachers and an Education Overhaul

Nicholas D. Kristof, a *New York Times* columnist, in a column republished in the Greensboro *News & Record* (January 13, 2012), pointed out the difference between a good teacher and a weak teacher over the life of a student. Kristof refers to a recent study by economists at Harvard and Columbia Universities to make his point. The study is noteworthy because "it involved a huge database of 1 million students following from fourth grade to adulthood." The blog of the Albert Shanker Institute, endorsed by the American Federation of Teachers (AFT), "praised the study as one of the most intense, important and interesting analysis on this topic in a very long time." The best teachers were identified and their students had significantly higher test scores and better life outcomes.

According to the three economists, Raj Chitty and John N. Friedman of Harvard and Jonah E. Rockoff of Columbia University, "each student in the class would have an extra accumulation of lifetime earnings of $52,000." The total gain in income per classroom would be $1.4 million. The authors of the study are of the opinion that "Our faltering education system may be the most important long-term threat to the United States economy and national well-being."

The solution from the study is to pay more for good teachers, which they define as 84 percent better than their peers. They recommend the elimination of weak teachers. Unfortunately, the authors of the study note that school reformers do not emphasize good teachers, but put the focus on the home because teachers can only do so much.

Like Joe Franks, I did not expect to teach. Instead I planned to join the Federal Bureau of Investigation for a career in criminal justice. However, the FBI required a law degree or an accounting degree and I decided to teach instead due to a lack of finances. My starting salary for 180 days of teaching was $1800 with a coaching supplement of $225 for the entire year.

North Carolina Teachers See 12 Percent Rate of Turnover in 2011

In 2011 teacher turnover increased slightly in North Carolina to one out of eight. However, "only 7 percent of these reported leaving because of a career change or because they were dissatisfied with teaching" (*News &Record*, Oct. 5, 2012). It is interesting to note that 21 percent of teachers leaving the profession came from retirement. Another 18 percent of teachers "resigned to teach elsewhere." Nine out of 10 moved in North Carolina or some other state and the rest to private or charter schools. Six percent left teaching for a career change and "less than 1 percent said they were resigning because they were fed up with the classroom environment" (*News & Record*, Oct. 5, 2012). State School Superintendent, June

Atkinson, commented on the status of teachers in 2012 when she said of the two reports:

> That's why we need to continue to give them the necessary support through good professional development, through good working conditions, through adequate compensation, in order to grow our profession (*News & Record*, Oct. 5, 2012).

The Scars Teachers Leave

Quintilian, a Roman educator, wrote, "Education is not what you are able to remember, but the things you can't forget." I can't forget several unfortunate things teachers did that stayed with me for all the years I taught at different times in my life.

How Did Washington Cross the Delaware?

I was a 7th grader in school in Newark, New Jersey. Our teacher came from a very affluent background, which was the opposite of my middle class, blue collar background. One day in American History class she got very emotional about George Washington crossing the ice filled waters to surprise the British forces across the Delaware River. She kept shouting, "How did he cross the river—how? How?" I turned to a classmate and jokingly said, "on ice skates." My friend laughed and she stopped everything and demanded to know what I said. When she heard what I said, she became emotional and took the next 40 minutes to humiliate me in front of the class. She called me a traitor to our country and told me I would go down in history with Benedict Arnold and other traitors in American History. She also told me that she planned to submit my name to the President of Harvard and the President of the University of Chicago to put in a book describing traitors to our country they were writing.

For several years I waited for the comments that would be published worldwide. I can't describe the shame I had and, as a real patriot, the scorn I would surely receive for my ill-fated remarks. I never confided in anyone about my attempt at humor, but suffered in silence instead. One night I heard Milton Berle, the comedian, make a similar remark on the radio. Only then did I believe I was not going down in American history as a despicable character. Needless to say, I chose to never embarrass or humiliate a student in front of a class I taught.

Lavinia, Put Your Head Down and Go to Sleep

As a Guilford College professor, I was asked to teach a group of 45 teachers in a graduate course for renewal credit at a neighboring university. The members of the class talked freely and we had lively discussions during the semester. Everyone talked with the exception of one woman who never said a word the entire semester. At the final session, I asked if anyone had anything they wanted to say before we ended the class. Suddenly, Lavinia said she wanted to say something (to the surprise of the entire class). She made several remarks and the class applauded her for her remarks. As I started to leave, she waited for me and said, "Listening to all the teachers, I realized that I was just as able to speak as anyone else. In fact, I talked yesterday in Sunday School class for the first time." She then told me her story and dilemma. In class one day, her favorite teacher asked her a question and she answered it for all to hear. She was shocked when her teacher said, "My God, Lavinia, that is really stupid. Put your head down on your desk and go to sleep." She continued, "From that day until this week, I never talked in public." I remember telling a teaching colleague that I would have taught that class without any compensation if I had known it would have changed a student's life and made such a difference.

You Must Have Cheated—It's Too Good

I was sitting at my kitchen table writing my doctoral dissertation when my son, a junior high school student, sat down and asked if I had some paper to write on. He proceeded to tell me his assignment in English was to write a myth. The myth was to be original and he could use his imagination. He loved Roman history and the many stories about Roman mythology. When he had finished I read what he had just written and told him it was exceptional and I was very impressed.

Several weeks passed and I remembered his paper. I asked if his teacher had commented and suddenly he got unexpectedly quiet. He said the teacher wrote on his paper that the myth was the best in the class. However, she wrote, "it was too good! You must have copied it from some other source." She gave him a C- and told him he was lucky she did not fail him. This was the same teacher who picked up a test paper in class and shouted to the others taking the test, "be careful, there is a cheater among us."

This was the same teacher who supervised one of my very good student teachers who was assaulted on the stairway and visibly disturbed. This teacher told our student teacher not to say anything to anyone, to keep the assault quiet!

These teachers were not the rule but the exception, yet they definitely left scars in the lives of their students. Never underestimate the impact that you can have on a person's life. Make sure your impacts are positive.

What Motivated You to Teach?

I once taught a summer class of students preparing for their terminal degrees who were exceptionally bright and eager to prepare to enter the teaching profession. One day I asked what motivated them to want to teach. To my surprise almost everyone said a teacher or a principal in high school had discouraged them by telling them that they were not capable of succeeding in college or in graduate work if they even graduated from college! They were determined because of the lack of faith by a teacher or administrator to make their life a success. Several said they actually took their college degree to the person who did not believe they could succeed in college. Again, scars were left, but the negative was always balanced by someone who believed in them and encouraged them.

At a recent North Carolina Sports Hall of Fame banquet, eight recipients of such an honor told of a person who was the reason for their success. It seems that this happens at every Hall of Fame ceremony. The good news is that there is always some teacher, coach, or administrator who had faith in them and made a difference in their life. Hopefully there are more special people who encouraged our young men and women than there were those who leave scars.

Another example of why teachers teach comes from Brooks Hamic White, a graduate student at Chowan University representing 30 women who were enrolled in the University's first master of arts degree in the school's long history. At the graduation ceremonies for these students who were elementary school teachers receiving their masters degrees, Brooks Hamic White made the graduation address to the group. She paid tribute to their professors and said:

> As Lauren Bacall once said: "Your heart is slightly bigger than the average human heart, but that is because you are a teacher." Our graduate cohort has had the honor and the privilege to be led by example, thank you for providing us with the knowledge to be nothing less than great ... Now, it's up to each one of us to make our great journey, our own difference (*USA Today*, Spring, Summer 2012).

In the write-up about her program, White made an impact on the group of teachers when she said:

> Our first day of graduate school began with our begging for fewer assignments and shortened class periods, and ended with our hanging onto knowledge that our peers have to offer in the form of a presentation or class discussion. We began by griping over reading assignments and ended thirsting for more. We began by rushing to our cars at the completion of class and ended by not wanting to leave (*CU Today*, Volume 64, Fall/Winter 2012).

These teachers learned the value and importance by having teachers that taught them to love learning that will extend into the rest of their lives.

JF:

Traditional Teaching Can Be Boring

Many of today's students are bored with traditional teaching techniques, so teachers have to be entertainers. Basically, as a teacher, you are on stage multiple times a day. You have in your mind a plan for what you want to accomplish, but many times, it is like being in an "improv" comedy club with audience participation. You have to learn the art of "winging it." Go with the flow of what the kids are giving you (although I did have a student tell me one time that only dead fish "go with the flow"). Get your students to pay attention—grab them and go on that learning journey. Some days you may get 45 minutes out of them, some days 25. And for the teachers out there who have to worry about student "time on task" in your evaluation, relax, there are creative ways to fill time and reinforce your lessons. The bottom line is that you want your students to learn and retain. Some of today's classrooms offer a myriad of electronic wizardry designed to engage students, but teachers shouldn't rely on technology to replace the human interaction that is so crucial to connecting with your students. Technology is NOT a crutch. In the 1980s, there were too many jokes in education about the VHS videotape being a "rectangular" lesson plan. Use technology as a tool to help illustrate, never to replace the essence of the lesson.

HA:

Why Our Kids Hate Math

Gary Thomas is a West Point graduate who teaches math at T.C. Williams High School in Alexandria, Virginia, along with colleague Sally Miller, who also teaches math. They believe there is a serious problem that leads to students hating math. The problem, according to Thomas and Miller, is that today's students in math are "pushed to the next level of math before they are ready." Students in their Algebra II class were placed there although "they slid by with D's in Algebra I and failed the state's Algebra I exam." According to Thomas and Miller:

> English and social studies teachers face the same problem when school officials, more interested in boasting about the numbers of kids in higher level courses than in what they really learn, place students without the requisite skills in advance placement classes.

Miller, like other math teachers, feels that pushing middle school students into algebra who are not developed mentally ready to deal with abstraction you can turn them off math forever.

Miller and Thomas caution all who push unprepared math students to a higher level of Algebra to remember that:

> It is time to ensure that all kids absorb the fundamentals of math—computation, fractions, percentages, decimals—first before moving on to the next level. Otherwise, as with remedial summer courses we're teaching them twice what they should have learned the first time around (*USA Today*, July 10, 2012).

School Is Too Easy, Students Report

A federal survey by the Center for American Progress, a "think tank that champions progressive ideas," analyzed three years of questionnaires from the Department of Education's National Assessment of Educational Progress, a national test given every year. Some of the findings include the following:

- 37 % of fourth-graders say their math work is too easy, often or always.
- 57% of eighth-graders say their history work is often or always too easy.
- 39% of twelfth-graders say they rarely write about what they read in class.

Shelby White, an English Education professor at Florida State University and a former classroom teacher said, "The curriculum is void of critical thinking, creative thinking. As a result students are probably bored and when they are bored they think the classes are easy." She puts this blame on "standardized tests that limit material teachers can cover" (*USA Today*, July 10, 2012).

Most Students Fail to Write Well

Mary Crovo, deputy director of the National Assessment Governing Board, said of test results taken by students for a Nation's Report Card:

> Students who have access to computers at home and regularly use them for assignments are more likely to be strong writers.

She reports, however, that a national test revealed that "Just a quarter of America's eighth and 12th grade students have solid writing skills" (*News & Record*, Sept, 15, 2012).

Crovo noted that "Students in both grades who used the thesaurus and backspace key more frequently had higher scores than those who used them less often." In addition, Crovo reports that "At the eighth grade, Asian students had the highest average score, which was 33 points higher than black students on a 300-point scale. At the 12th grade, white students scored 27 points above black students" (*News & Record*, Sept. 15, 2012).

JF:

Teach to Retain — Not "To the Test"

In my experience, I have found the greatest way to enhance retention — repetition. Sure, we all know this but can we put it into effective practice? Haven't you noticed that some students can't remember quotes, facts, or general information but they can go down the hall singing or rapping and get all the words in correct sequence every time. Of course, part of this ability relates to motivation — they will do what they enjoy. Yet I feel that the fact they listen to songs over and over is essential to the memory process. Over the years I have developed what I call an evaluation cycle that we complete for each unit—and I got the original idea from a cousin of mine who was a science teacher for over 30 years. Folks, it is fellowship and exchange of ideas with fellow teachers that have the greatest impact on our craft—not some workshop where the instructor is paid mega-bucks to talk about some paradigm shift that may be on the horizon.

By the time students take one of my tests, they have: 1) read over a selected chapter and had a short quiz on that reading (that is how you get them to skim it—give them a quiz!); 2) have had a homework assignment to identify key terms and concepts; 3) have had a recall (memory) quiz on some of those terms; 4) have taken notes and had class discussion; 5) had a major matching quiz on their terms, reading and notes two days prior to the major test. I know it sounds like a lot of time, but it really is easily incorporated into daily lessons and kids know what to expect week to week. By the time the test comes around, it should be easy because they know the material. I have found that when students complain that a test was really hard, it is either because they have not prepared properly or that the material was not taught efficiently. Make your tests easy by TEACHING THE MATERIAL in ways that students can easily retain. Pound it in there over and over. Make it automatic—give them associations through connections or mnemonics. Their scores will improve, their enjoyment of learning will improve and your satisfaction will improve. Give it a shot.

HA:

Security on School Testing Called Lax

The *Atlanta Journal-Constitution* surveyed 50 state education departments and found "that most do not use the basic test security measures designed to prevent cheating" (*News & Record*, Oct.

1, 2012). The survey also found that almost half of the states make no attempt "to screen the test results for irregularities."

The *Journal-Constitution* reported early this year that over 200 school districts had not discovered suspicious changes in test scores. The No Child Left Behind Act "made standardized testing the conversation of national education policy." Education Secretary Arne Duncan said that test security is left to the states. Most states assign the investigations of cheating to school districts and the federal government has no standards to protect the integrity of the achievement tests in the thousands of schools required to test their students. Critics of the required testing under the No Child Left Behind Act are not sure that the important test scores are legitimate. The lack of security is blamed for the cheating scandals in Atlanta, Philadelphia, Columbus, Ohio, El Paso, Texas and other cities (*News & Record*, Oct. 1, 2012).

I Have to Teach to the Test to Keep My Job

John Horshok, recently named Executive Director of the Harmon Killebrew Foundation, joined me in volunteering to teach in a sports marketing class at a nearby secondary school. We invited 17 outstanding people, who represent every area of sports, to speak to our two classes of 25 students each. We planned to engage our students in discussions, moral dilemmas, videos and other technological aids with an emphasis on critical thinking.

Our lead teacher in this unique class was excellent, possessing a thorough background in teaching business and management courses. She welcomed our ideas but told us that she had to teach from the book assigned her so that the class would have high scores on the final examination designed by the state. She made it clear that she would not be retained to teach if the test scores for the course were low.

We were extremely disappointed, but we understood her dilemma and wanted to cooperate with her. It became clear to us that innovation would be stifled and wondered if we could be effective for the year-round course. We decided to try as best we could to utilize as many of our ideas as possible, but still not hinder her plans to meet her obligation.

Cheating Scandals Result from No Child Left Behind Program

Fannie Flono, a columnist for the *Charlotte Observer*, described teaching for the test as begetting cheating and failing. I was reminded of my college days at Wake Forest, which had a zero tolerance for anyone caught cheating—an honor code that worked. I remember how afraid I was to look anywhere but on my test paper, and looked straight ahead so that I would not be accused of cheating.

During my years at Wake Forest, I was elected to the Judicial Board, the board that heard cases involving cheating. We wore robes during hearings when a student was turned in and tried for suspected cheating of any kind. It was sad and often traumatic to try a pre-medical student who was brought before us for an honor code violation. When the Judicial Board found the student guilty of a violation of the Honor Code, an automatic "F" was assigned for the course. It was mandatory. This almost always meant the person's degree and opportunity to get into medical school was over. It was always a traumatic experience in our lives as well as that of the person who was found guilty.

Flono writes:

> Today, the litany of revelations and allegations of how some teachers have aided and engaged in test cheating themselves is the scary part. Recent reports that a whopping 178 Atlanta public school teachers and principals—82 of them who have confessed—took part in the cheating scandal.

Following the Atlanta cheating scandal, Philadelphia initiated an investigation after 89 schools, 28 in the city, "had received questionable gains on test scores." For decades test scores have been investigated concerning cheating, including schools in Washington, D.C., Arizona, California, Florida, Maryland, Michigan, New Jersey, New York, Ohio, Texas, Pennsylvania and Georgia.

Much of the blame for the cheating was placed on the "No Child Left Behind" program that emphasized test scores that resulted in schools being labeled good or bad. It also "threatened loss of funding or other punitive measures if students weren't proficient in math and reading by 2014."

Atlanta teachers talked of their fear that low test scores would affect their livelihood. In addition to this fear of the impact on low scores, the teachers also had an incentive for merit pay if the test scores were high. A teacher and principal in Washington, D.C. allegedly received a bonus of $12,000 for raising test scores.

Flono concluded:

> These scandals are no substitute for teaching. Tests should be diagnostic tools to help students address their weaknesses and master material. And given all of the factors outside of the classroom that affect student learning, tests are an insufficient gauge of a teacher's impact on performance (*News & Record*, Jan. 14, 2011).

Benefits of No Child Left Behind Program

Former North Carolina Governor Beverly Perdue visited a class in Konnoak Elementary School in Winston-Salem, North Carolina, where No Child Left Behind is implemented. The school's principal selected Heather Stanley-Johnson's class of pre-kindergarten children. Johnson's classes have been a model for the program, one that starts with many children who are just learning the English language.

In an interview on October 8, 2012, Johnson had this to say about the program's attempt to involve parents in the education program for their children. "One of the strong points about the parental involvement is the fact that the children quickly began to speak and write in English, and help their parents begin to become proficient in English as a result of their children's involvement with the English language." In addition, Heather Johnson describes the support their children receive from the program in pointing out:

> Parents of children enrolled in the program are welcome anytime they choose to visit. Whenever possible parents are strongly encouraged to actively participate by volunteering. At least 3 hours a month are requested

for the program. We have a volunteer book in the classroom with each child's hours documented. Some ideas include, but are not limited to, reading to and with children, playing in the dramatic play area, coaching art work, playing games on the playground, building blocks and assisting in tabletop games. Parent meetings are held throughout the year with notices posted and sent home. Home visits are conducted twice during the school year. To establish a relationship with the family, give specific information about the curriculum and general program information.

Lastly, family/parent meetings are held throughout the year based on parent interest. Some topics might include developmentally appropriate practices for preschoolers, positive discipline and literacy activities.

Heather Johnson recognizes much of the good in the No Child Left Behind pre-K programs. Parents come into her classroom with their pre-K child. She feels that the parents become involved with their child's education by talking with her and knowing what their child is doing. She noted that one half of her class cannot speak English, but adapt rapidly to English. She also said that the parents begin to speak English because of their children who pick it up and quickly help them begin to speak and write more effectively.

Heather Johnson welcomes her interaction with the parents, which is one of the No Child Left Behind benefits. She sees problems with the entire program, but believes the pre-K emphasis makes a positive difference with her young children. She said:

I have always believed that what I am inside is what helps me make and do everything in life. My goal as an early childhood educator is to make the most of each day students spend in my care, respecting individual differences and student learning by considering special learning needs. By encouraging all of the learning styles and needs in the classroom, I can create balance and unity within the content areas. In addition, provide instructional improvement through planning rich experiences that offer a variety of opportunities for children to learn new skills and knowledge. Every child will demonstrate varying degrees of strengths in their domains and all children are capable of positive achievements. It is only through appropriate early childhood learning practices that rigorous early learning standards can be implemented and achieved (North Carolina Guide for the Early Years, 2009).

She also pointed out that

Appropriate practice is about how children learn, the competence of the teachers and the involvement of the family and community collaboration to support each child's learning and development. My classroom combines high expectations for each child with respect for individual differences and this is why I believe Governor Perdue came to visit Konnoak Elementary School, family fun activities, and transition to Kindergarten (Interview with Heather Johnson, November 25, 2012).

Quit Fretting: U.S. Doing OK for Science Education

Alex Berezow and Hank Campbell, authors of the forthcoming book, *Science Left Behind*, discuss the criticism that "our once, unchallenged pre-eminence in commerce, industry, science and technological innovation is being overtaken by competitors throughout the world" (*USA Today*, June 4, 2012). The authors point out that:

A recent National Assessment of Educational Progress science test, given to eighth graders, showed a statistically significant increase in scores in 2009 where 63% of all students had a basic grasp of science. In 2011, the total increased to 65%. Scores for minorities improved the most. This upward trend is encouraging news.

Part of the problem, the authors say, is that in 1964 the first standardized tests were given on an international test. Americans finished next to last. In 2009, the U.S. finished 17th out of 34 countries. Many critics admit that Americans do not do well on standardized tests.

The authors note:

> the achievement during this period of mediocrity when we created the Silicon Valley, built multinational biotechnology firms and continued to lead the world in scientific publications and total number of Nobel Prize winners we also invented and sold more than a few iPads. Obviously standardized tests aren't everything.

Finally the authors point out that:

> Be wary of education lobbyists who downplay our long track record of scientific success while asking for more money. At $591,700 per pupil from kindergarten through twelve grades, the U.S. is outspent only by Switzerland in the education arena. Cash is not the problem.

Universitas 21, a global network of research universities concluded:

> The United States ranks No 1 in the world in higher education. Sweden came in a distant second (*USA Today*, June 4, 2012).

And Daniel A. Domenech, Executive Director of the American Association of School Administrators (AASA) writes in the January 2012 edition of *eSchool News*,

> The fact that we have to defend public education in the first place is puzzling. Here we sit as the most powerful country in the world, with the largest economy, and the system responsible now for the education of close to 90 percent of our children is under attack.

America's Public School System Is Still Strong

Domenech developed a Power/Point presentation named the *95/5 Dilemma* available on the AASA website at http://www.aasa.org/AASAblog-95-5dilemma.aspx. In it he provides statistic after statistic to prove that American education is still the best in the world. He writes:

> America's public school system is the best it has ever been. Graduation rates are the highest. Drop-out rates are the lowest. Reading and math performances on the National Assessment of Education Progress are the highest. College attendance rates are the highest. The rigor of the high school curriculum is the strongest ever (*eSchool News*, January 2012).

Domenech describes the comments of educators world-wide when he travels and the reality that the educators all over the world refer to our educational system as the "Gold Standard." They reportedly want to send their children to be educated in the United States. Recently, South Korea announced that "they will replace paper textbooks with electronic tablets that have customized e-learning systems by 2014."

One of the reasons for change by the South Koreans is to narrow the gap between the poor and the affluent. In addition, "they want to make learning fun and effective."

It is clear that Asians envy our creativity and want to include it in their educational process (*News & Record*, July 24, 2011).

Teacher Education a Key

Like Joe Franks, Domenech believes that we can learn from others ways to improve and modify America's public schools. One powerful suggestion is that we should continue to work with our teachers after they enter the teaching profession. Teacher development is one of the specific goals of educators, not something that ends when they graduate from college. Many educators believe that the quality of the teacher is the most important variable in getting children to learn (*eSchool News*, January 2012).

The problem appears to be evident: "We do not spend the time or the money to fully develop our teachers."

Domenech concludes with renewed hope for improving America's educational system by advocating teacher evaluations that recognize both the outstanding teacher as well as those who need help with their teaching skills.

Domenech concludes that America will do well to "appreciate cultures—that have a high regard for education and the educators who provide it." He notes that he believes traveling to other countries makes one proud to be educators in America (*eSchool News*, January 2012).

JF:

Passion Is the Key to Great Teaching

One characteristic of a great teacher is passion. Get excited and enthusiastic about what you do. If you get excited and project that what you are doing is cool, kids feed off that. And make sure you let them know some of what you are passionate about in life. As I said before, Clemson University had a great impact on my life and career. I have held onto my love of Clemson and it shows in my classroom, my clothes, my car—in essence, my life. The kids know this and feed off it. At school, many students simply know me as "the crazy Clemson guy," and that's okay. When my team wins, they know I'm in a good mood, and when they get beat, students understand that I can take some good natured "ribbing" from them as well. I even get heckled from kids in the hallways I don't even have in class! Another great thing you can do is get involved in "spirit days" at school. Dress up with other teachers and show the students that it is cool to be involved and have spirit. That means a lot to them.

HA:

Passion for Learning: A Key to True Education

Just as teachers need to be passionate about teaching, students need to be passionate for true education. Vishal Khanna in writing about passion for learning on the part of our students believes it is extremely important. Joe Franks insists that as teachers we must have a passion for teaching if we are to be effective motivators in the quest to have students who have an overwhelming desire to learn.

Khanna explains that many educators debate the effectiveness of homework. He recognizes the need for some homework, but writes that "the wrong types of homework do nothing good for a child." He believes that "They drain children of their desire to learn and strip them of the beauty and sanctity of learning for learning's sake." Khanna believes that our current educational system prevents students who are pushed by teachers who teach to the test, to become "commodified and packaged into the anathema of true mentorship which to him is giving a child the tools to think for himself/herself and sharing with him or her a passion for knowledge and wisdom."

He concludes on the value of passion by teachers and students of learning by passion when he writes:

> We can compete in the world, as individuals and as a nation, only through passion and only through ingenuity. Without those, we will fail and we will be left behind (*News & Record*, June 29, 2012).

JF:

Have a Goal to Make a Difference

While there is no such thing as an indispensable person, you can make yourself very valuable to your school by making your school a better place because you are there—make it your goal to make a difference! That is a piece of advice that I try to instill in my students. A great way to enhance your teaching and connect with students is to make sure they see you outside the classroom. Get involved on your campus. Be a club advisor or learn to coach. I know in my heart that because of my involvement in athletics, leading spirit assemblies, and being visible on campus it has helped me be a better teacher because it has created a more personal relationship with students. Anyone who has taught for a few years knows how funny it is to hear kids talk about seeing one of their teachers at the "grocery store" or just out shopping—like teachers don't have a life outside of the school. When students get to see teachers outside what they consider the "normal" realm of our existence, it makes an impression. Even the students you don't teach hear about your exploits from the others. The bottom line here is that you need to make that positive connection with the young people in your school. One needs to walk that fine line between running a taut ship in the classroom and connecting on a personal level with the students you teach. Have standards and hold them accountable with consequences, but do it in a consistent and fair way. They will respond to that. When discipline is equitable for all, students deal with it very well. After a period of time, don't be afraid to share your personal thoughts, opinions and concerns with them. Let them see the person—not just the "teacher." Learn from them like they learn from you—experience education together.

HA:

Our Schools Need a Few Good Men

William Gromley, a professor at the Georgetown Public Policy Institute and co-director of the Center for Research on Children in the United States, commented on teachers in the United States today. Gormley, the author of *Voices for Children: Rhetoric and Public Policy*, made the following observations concerning the status of teachers:

> Studies show that years of good teaching can set a student on a good path, while years of bad teaching can do the opposite.

One of the problems the U.S. faces is the fact that:

> Only a fraction of our teachers are the best and brightest of their generation. According to a 2010 McKinsey report, nearly half of U.S. teachers come from the bottom third of their class (*USA Today*, August 14, 2012).

Gormley believes that we have a problem that needs attention — a lack of male teachers. He reports that:

> Teachers dominate the profession especially in the pre-K and kindergarten teachers where only 2 percent are men. In elementary and middle schools, 18 percent are men. However, in secondary schools, 42 percent are men (Bureau of Labor Statistics, 2012).

According to Gormley, "men represent an underutilized talent pool." He doesn't believe "that men are better teachers, but that highly qualified men are far less likely to apply for teaching jobs."

Thomas Dee, a Stanford University professor, conducted a study of 20,000 middle-school boys and found that "boys perform better when they have a male teacher — we especially need more black male teachers in the classroom."

Education Secretary, Arne Duncan has argued "all of our students benefit from having a black male in the classroom. But particularly our young black males" (*USA Today*, August 14, 2012).

JF:

Secretary Duncan and others need look no further than my alma mater Clemson University. An innovative program called Call Me Mister has been in place at Clemson for many years that has the purpose of training young African American males to be educators in the primary grades. One of my good friends, who was an All American at Clemson and member of the college football Hall of Fame, Jeff Davis, was the Field Director and public face of this program when Oprah Winfrey decided to have Jeff on the program and make a financial contribution. Since its inception in 1998, the Call Me Mister program has spread throughout colleges and universities in South Carolina and has expanded to institutions of higher learning in seven other states. As of fall 2012, the program has graduated 86 Misters and the number will grow each year.

HA:

Finally, Gromley gives several recommendations for attracting more males to the profession:

1. Schools of Education should aggressively recruit male applicants.
2. Teach for America should target male applicants.
3. Strengthen the Troops for Teachers to increase the number of veterans who are males.
4. Higher wages for teachers will help.

In conclusion, Gromley said:

> We need to be more creative in letting young men know that they should consider teaching as a profession (*USA Today*, August 14, 2012).

JF:

Extracurricular Activities Are Crucial in the Educational Process

For many of today's students, the fun and enjoyment of school is either a thing of the past—or worse, something they have never experienced. This is unfortunate and unnecessary. I firmly believe that young people can learn and have a great time doing it. I also believe that if you get students to invest in their school—through clubs, the arts and athletics—it provides a well-rounded educational experience for them. Unfortunately, because politicians and educational bureaucrats have become obsessed with test scores, they are often blinded to the benefits of many extracurricular programs. Additionally, in tough economic times when hard budget decisions have to be made the bureaucrats usually pick the extracurriculars like the arts and athletics—things that make education enjoyable for students and motivate some to stay to school in the first place. When I was in school, being involved in the choir and as a student trainer provided great satisfaction and enjoyment. As a teacher who has been involved in athletics since I returned to my alma mater as a nationally certified athletic trainer and now as a coach, I have a good perspective on what involvement, particularly in athletics, does for kids. The life skills, the social skills, and team building learned through athletics are unmatched in the educational environment.

HA:

The Case for High School Activities

The National Federation of State High School Associations (NFHS) believes, like the authors, "interscholastic sports and fine arts activities promote citizenship and sportsmanship. They instill a sense of pride in community and teach lifelong lessons of teamwork."

The NFHS conducted a survey of extracurricular activities and published its results in the Fall of 2011. The outstanding report can be obtained through its Power Point and videos on a CD. (To obtain a copy call 800-776-3462.)

NFHS lists the benefits of co-curricular activities as follows:

1. Activities support the academic mission of schools.
2. Activities are inherently educational.
3. Activities foster success in later life.

A Harvard Educational Review (2002) reported several statistics that reveal the importance of these activities such as:

1. Students who spend no time in extracurricular activities are 49% more likely to use drugs.
2. The study found that participation in these activities appear to be one of the few interventions that benefit low status, disadvantaged students—those less well served by

traditional educational programs — as much more than their more advantaged peers.

The NFHS report goes on to make positive comments about participation in activities citing:

1. Students who compete in high school activity programs make higher grades and have better attendance.
2. Participation in activity programs yields positive results after high school as well.
3. From a cost standpoint, activity programs are an exceptional bargain when matched against the overall school district education budget.
4. Activity programs fulfill students' basic needs, help students' attitudes toward self and school and minimize dropout and discipline problems.
5. Co-curricular activities teach lessons that lead to better citizens.

The Women's Sports Foundation, in a 1989 nationwide study, concluded:

1. Girls receive as many benefits from sports as boys.
2. The "dumb jock" stereotype is a myth.
3. Sports involvement was significantly related to a drop-out rate in some school settings.
4. Minority athletes are more socially involved than non-athletes.

The NFHS report compared athletes with non-athletes in grade point average, attendance, discipline referrals, drop-out and graduation rates and found from several studies that activity involved students performed better in every classification.

The NFHS report utilized study after study on a national basis for their outstanding report and should be required reading for anyone interested in the multi-studies regarding the benefits of extracurricular activities in the schools of the United States.

Are Sports Educational?

In Vol. 23, No. 2 of *From the Gym to the Jury*, Dr. Tom Appenzeller asked the readers to respond to a very important question a college student asked him. Appenzeller stated that he did not believe he could answer the following question a student posed to him: Are interscholastic and intercollegiate sports educational or extracurricular? Barbara Osborne, Associate Professor of Exercise and Sport Science at the University of North Carolina at Chapel Hill, provided important insight:

> In response to your question "are interscholastic and intercollegiate sports educational or extra-curricular?" The simple answer is "yes." You are completely correct in the variety of examples used in your front-page commentary from the V.23 (2) issue of *From the Gym to the Jury*. However, you tried to mix a variety of legal theories in providing your examples. I remind my students all the time that the law is not like a giant buffet that you can pick and choose any combination you like. Using your Title IX example: Title IX is a statute, and courts will examine the plain meaning of the legislation as well as any legislative history or legislative intent in interpreting it's meaning. Courts are also deferential to the administrative agency (in this case, the US Department of Education) regulations, if there are any. So when examining whether interscholastic and/or intercollegiate sports are "an educational program or activity" within the context of Title IX, the courts look at the various OCR regulations, policy interpretations, and clarifications. It is clear that these programs are educational within the meaning of this statute. When you move to constitutional law, there are different tests for equal protection and due process claims. Staying with the gender theme, a claim that female athletes are discriminated against in violation of the equal protection clause will merit intermediate

scrutiny by the courts. This requires the court to determine whether the allegedly discriminatory rule or action is justifiable because it is substantially related to an important government interest. Because equal protection is a constitutional law claim, there must be state action (whereas Title IX is broader reaching because it is spending clause legislation affecting any school, public or private, that receives federal funding). Under equal protection it doesn't matter whether athletics is extra curricular or educational. Due process is also a constitutional law claim (and therefore requires state action), but there must be a life, liberty or property interest in order for due process to be implicated. Here, as you noted, the majority of courts have found that there is no liberty or property interest in participating in interscholastic or intercollegiate athletics. These decisions are made on a state by state basis, so whether athletics is an extra-curricular privilege that receives no due process protection or a part of a student's education which might be a right provided by a state constitution, will depend upon the precedent established in that state. From a procedural due process perspective, even if a court finds that interscholastic athletics is educational and a liberty or property right, it would likely merit minimum due process protection. If an athlete is prohibited from playing, they likely have already received notice and the opportunity to speak on their behalf, so minimum due process would be satisfied, the school wins and the athlete still can't play. From a substantive due process perspective, there still has to be a life, liberty, or property interest at stake before the court will examine whether or not a rule is fundamentally fair. Even in the few states that might recognize a liberty or property interest in athletics as education, the courts are extremely deferential to the school's authority, rather than substitute the courts judgment for that of education professionals. The Vernonia v. Acton example raises another Constitutional law claim: a violation of the Fourth Amendment prohibition against unreasonable searches and seizures. Again, there are unique legal elements for the court to examine for a search and seizure claim including whether or not the search is reasonable both in its scope and at its inception. If the search is reasonable, then the court will balance the individual's privacy interests against the government's interest to render a final decision. Due process is invoked in these cases in order to make this federal constitutional requirement applicable to the states. Because an athletics eligibility situation is a state matter, we're back to determining whether there is a recognizable life, liberty or property interest. Fortunately, privacy is a recognized liberty interest, so it doesn't matter whether or not athletics participation is extra-curricular or educational. I hope that I've sufficiently answered your (student's) question. The law is not inconsistent not contradictory, and the courts are applying the tests and precedent relevant to a particular legal claim within a specific legal theory.

Opportunity Gap Growing between Rich and Poor Children

David Brooks, a columnist for the *New York Times*, writes about Robert Putnam, a Harvard political scientist and his latest study. Putnam and his team of researchers found research they called "horrifying." Putnam's group "looked at inequality of opportunity among children." The data of Putnam's research verify "that children of the more affluent are raised in starkly different ways and have different opportunities."

Putnam's research found that affluent parents invest more time than parents with low income. College education parents spend time talking to their children about their day in school and cheer them on from the sidelines. Parents with a high school education do not spend as much time with their children as they did years ago. Over the last 40 years, parents with a college education spend money to enrich activities such as "tutoring and extracurricular opportunities" by $5,300 a year compared to $480 for parents with high school education.

Putnam's research reveals that richer kids are roughly more likely to play after-school sports. They are more than twice as likely to be the captains of their sports teams. They are much more likely to do non-sports activities, like theater, yearbook and scouting. They are much more likely to attend religious services. Putnam notes that:

> It is perfectly understandable that kids from working class backgrounds have become cynical and even paranoid, for virtually all our majors social institutions have failed them—family, friends, church, school and community.

He further comments that "As a nation we must address the problem or as a nation we will commit 'national suicide'" (*News & Record*, July 11, 2012).

As a nation we made equal opportunity the core to our nation's identity and asked that politicians both liberal and conservative be willing to "take advantage of all its human capital rather than the most privileged." Politicians must work together to attempt to address the problem rather than take positions that divide our country.

JF:

I'm a Teacher, and Proud of It

While teaching is an admirable and wonderful profession, it can also be one of the most misunderstood. I can't tell you how frustrating it is to be in a social situation, talk about professions and have some idiot say in a very condescending way, "Oh, so you teach"—like I could get a "real" job. You know something, my job happens to be one of the most critical in this society, and if society realized that we would be much better off in the long run. I have the opportunity to touch lives and hopefully make a difference—that's the goal. At the beginning of each new school year, I tell my students that I want this to be the best class they have all day long—and I mean it. Yet if this profession is so great, and I believe that it is, why do so many good people get out of it so quickly? Why is there so much teacher turnover? The cold, hard fact is that teachers are not necessarily treated like professionals. There are times when we feel that we are not supported and the work environment can be unbearable.

A major, if not THE major concern, relates to student discipline and the apparent non-support of administrators. How can a teacher get something accomplished when many students in class are so unruly or one who tells a teacher "F_ _ _ You" is sent to the office, only to return to the same classroom 20 minutes later after a "stern" talking to by an administrator? When this lack of support occurs, it is no wonder that people say goodbye to teaching. And please don't respond to this by saying something like, "Well, if the teacher had appropriate discipline in that class, this would never happen!" These types of situations happen at all levels regardless of school circumstances. Yet, I believe these are correctable problems that I will address later with some operational ideas for educational improvement. The bottom line is that people don't leave teaching because of low pay, they leave teaching because of a poor work environment. Improve the work environment and you will retain more and better teachers—and the education of students will improve dramatically.

Chapter 3

Character Education
Is Important

JF:

A few years ago, our system had a superintendent who began a character education initiative that a subsequent superintendent did not value and thus let the program lapse. From the initial character education program, there were posters that listed some "cornerstones" of character. Having some extras, I gave them to some coaches to put in their locker rooms because the positive message made sense — these were the kind of traits that one would hope their athletes would develop not only to be better team members, but to be good citizens and role models for others. Talk about cross-curricular influence with a program — this was golden! Involvement in athletics is educational and should be encouraged. Unfortunately, educational bureaucrats take pride in singling out athletes and coaches to show how tough they are on athletes. This is a sham! Check out the "Case for High School Athletics" put out by the North Carolina High School Athletic Association (NCHSAA). You can find it online at http://www.nchsaa.org/page.php?mode=privateview&pageID=49. This study shows what many of us in scholastic athletics already know too well. Students who are involved in extracurricular athletics have better attendance, fewer discipline problems, better grades and a higher graduation rate than their counterparts who are not involved. In fact, the National College Athletic Association (NCAA) has used a television commercial that basically says the same thing—that athletes perform academically as well or better in some cases as their peers. So why are barriers created in some school districts to make it more difficult to participate in athletics? Give me the rationale that justifies singling out student-athletes and holding them accountable to higher academic standards than the general student body? Specifically, the trend in some districts is to make athletes have a 2.0 grade point average to participate. If this 2.0 average is so important, why not make it a graduation requirement? In North Carolina, we have common sense athletic eligibility at the state level that basically says that a student athlete must pass a minimum number of classes, and be in school for at least 85 percent each semester. In addition, they obviously have to meet local promotional standards. If students meet these requirements, they will be on course to graduate, and isn't that the goal of high school students—to receive a diploma? I am constantly amazed at bureaucrats who want to lump extra on kids who are involved and doing what they should to be on course to graduate. Don't penalize them and put hurdles before them; try to get more kids to be like them!

HA:

Character Education

When I was in high school in the early 1940s, we had a course called "civics." In this semester-long class, we talked about our form of government. Its values, laws and what amounted to today's Character Education, and it was a required course. Citizenship was stressed with an emphasis on the student's role in society. Today, we call it by other names, but Character Education seems to be the one most used.

My wife, Ann Terrill Appenzeller, a political science major at the College of William and Mary, and I applied for a grant from the Smith Richardson Foundation to work with teachers in Law-Related Education (Character Education now). Along with the Law-Related Section of the State Department of Education, the teachers would be selected from kindergarten to the 12th grade to experience Law-Related Education and receive a stipend to attend. Our grant was approved, and we were ready to try new approaches to old practices we believed were important for students of all grade-levels.

We were pleased when a large number of teachers applied for the Law-Related Education program that would be one week in duration at Guilford College. Our group was housed and fed in the residence halls at the college. We invited attorneys, judges, law professors, all outstanding resources, and included police-ride-alongs for the benefit of the participants. The curriculum was challenging and innovative to the teachers. We learned many lessons from the week-long seminars and community leaders who were excited to be a part of the innovative program.

One experience we had during the week was not embraced by several teachers at the primary and elementary level. They were opposed to the police ride-alongs. We emphasized that the program was voluntary and no one had to go on the ride-alongs. The response to the activity was overwhelming and so enthusiastic that the teachers who chose not to go changed their minds. At our evaluation sessions, teachers who at first chose not to go confessed that they were so impressed with the police that they completely changed their negative attitude toward the police. They admitted that even in the primary grades they had been guilty of putting police down to their young students. They were determined to place the police in a positive light to their students from that day on.

The conference on Law-Related Education was one of the best ventures we experienced and the grantors were excited over the results, for many represented a complete change of attitude and excitement about education. This program continued for several years and we would hope that similar workshops will continue in the future.

Your Character Compass

"Successful leadership is not about being tough or soft, sensitive or assertive, but about a set of attributes. First and foremost is character" (Warren Bennis). Jim Scifres, a counselor and speaker on character education, speaking on the importance of character and integrity in the 21st century, questioned a person's character compass. He asked:

> Is your character compass pointing to true north? Are you conducting your affairs and doing business in a way that will be a positive model, one that will be admired, trusted, and widely respected? (*Character 21*, July 13, 2009)

Character … Becoming Cheapened and Devalued

Good character, once applauded and respected, is becoming cheapened and devalued at an alarming rate. Compromises in character and integrity have become more common-place; causing society to expect it, and to be more accepting of it. Slanted media coverage is causing us to become numb and desensitized to a grave situation that needs our utmost attention. We are on a slippery slope that is steadily leading society to a cultural shift in values (*Character 21*, July 13, 2009).

Chapter 4

Educational Experts and Their Unintended Consequences

JF:

Let me be candid with my thoughts about educational bureaucrats and school administrators—the really good ones are few and far between. When you can find a school administrator who exhibits good people skills and leads with common sense and a dose of reality—thank the Lord. Just because something seems to be a good idea doesn't mean it is. We have seen too many examples of programs resulting in unintentional consequences that are detrimental to students, schools and our society. And many of these decisions might have been avoided or adjusted if the bureaucrats and administrators actually asked TEACHERS to provide input on the ideas.

Let me give some shining examples of "Great Decisions in Education." (This would be perfect with the theme from Anheuser-Busch's "Real Men of Genius" ad campaign.) A generation ago, when educational bureaucrats chose to focus of academic achievement to the exclusion of all else, they made a decision to deemphasize physical education in the schools—what a tragic decision. Today, we have study after study that reveals that our youth are the most out of shape, poorly nourished, overweight kids ever. Not to mention the fact that related health problems like diabetes are on the rise among young people. And the educational bureaucrats are still reluctant to make real physical education a priority in the schools. I'll bet many of these "educational leaders" have family health club memberships and the like, but wouldn't it be nice if we could instill a healthful living component to education that creates a lifestyle for young people that may continue into adulthood. Wouldn't that be good for our society? But it has nothing to do with academic rigor, so it is low on the priority chart. I applaud the NFL and their promotion of the "Play 60" initiative, and we have politicians talking about healthy living. But from an educational perspective, what are we really doing to promote physical activity and require it in our schools? Seems to me we are only concerned about updating nutrition guidelines, not curricular requirements that encourage and require daily physical activity.

On a more local level from what I have experienced through the years, I've got some great ones. When I was 15, I took driver's education in school. One of my coaches was my teacher, and I can still remember components from the class portion and especially the driving instruction during the school day. This was complete instruction, a class with a grade. Well, a few years ago the State of North Carolina decided that driver's education was not appropriate for the academic curricula in school. Whether this was motivated by misguided academicians or bureaucrats looking to privatize the program to save money, this was an ill-advised idea. So, goodbye driver's education, and enter the private driving schools. What we have come to see since this approach was adopted is that the quality of driving of young people in North Carolina has deteriorated to the point where we now have to have more restricted and graduated licenses for young drivers. I understand that my rationale may be simplistic, but take a common sense view of what was done and what has happened! Quality instruction was taken away from TEACHERS, and thus we have now had to legislate restrictions because of what is not being done with regard to driver instruction in our state.

The Middle School Concept Needs Modification

From attending my high school in a 10th–12th grade format, and returning to teach there after graduating from college, when it was still a 10th–12th grade school, I really believed that having 9th graders in high school would be beneficial to the overall school climate. I felt that the 9th graders were probably a little "big" for junior high and that they would successfully integrate gradually into the expanded high school format. Unfortunately, I have come to see that there is a disproportionate number of discipline issues and suspensions with the freshmen in the system. I have never taught in a middle school, and my hat is off to the folks who do, but what I do see is the end result of what I believe is a flawed middle school concept. From what I am told and what I have observed, a key emphasis of the middle school concept is building the self-esteem of the students in middle school. On the surface, that's fine. Kids need to feel good about themselves, but they also have to learn accountability and responsibility. I see freshmen coming to high school each year who have an over-inflated opinion of themselves, cannot follow directions, and don't feel that they should be accountable for any of their behavior. Therefore, we deal with these issues at the high school level, which hinders the successful transition to high school for some. Instead of addressing issues of accountability and responsibility at a younger age, dealing with these issues as a learning component of the middle school, our system has added extra counselors and administrators to deal exclusively with the "challenges" of the 9th graders. There was even talk of segregating 9th grade classes into an on-campus "academy" to help them "transition into the high school environment." Boy, that makes sense to put a band-aid on the problem instead of dealing with it proactively at the source and helping these students be more responsible BEFORE they get to the high school level. With regard to the hierarchy of educational transition in our country, pre-school needs to prepare children for elementary school, elementary school needs to prepare children for middle school, and middle school needs to prepare students for high school—end of story. Our high schools need to prepare young adults to either continue their education, enter the work force or join the military. Our educational system needs to ensure that our high school graduates become productive members of our society, now and in the future.

Tracking

Students have been, and will continue to be placed/tracked into classes based on ability and academic performance. The term tracking is out of favor in today's educational environment because it has been seen as discriminatory. Some students are placed in higher, more challenging classes, while others are stigmatized by being in lower level classes. When I first started teaching in the fall of 1983, I taught a class called United States History Workshop for juniors and seniors in high school who read below a 5th grade level. Let's not debate how these students got into the 11th grade. These classes were needed—you have to meet students where they are and give them a chance to succeed. The bottom line is that these classes worked—they gave students basic competencies and knowledge in history. Then came along the paradigm that all schools need to do is challenge children and they will rise to higher levels. Mainstream them into higher level classes and they will perform—raise the bar and they will get to it. Yes, some may, but this sink-or-swim mentality created situations where students who did not have the foundation or ability fell behind, became frustrated and failed to succeed—this leads to dropouts! Folks, teachers are like potters—you have to have moldable clay to create works of art. When students lack basic competencies, you must give instruction that meets their needs. When all children rise because they developed and achieved competencies at every level, you can do away with lower level instruction. But until that time, meet them where they are! This will take time, but will eventually become unnecessary when 8th, 10th and 12th graders are performing at expected levels. As the idea of "tracking" students fell out of favor, lower level classes were eliminated, or at least that was the claim. In our district, the workshop class was simply dropped from the curriculum. I was against this for the very reasons I have listed above—if we have kids that were at this level, we should have suitable and appropriate instruction for their needs. For many reasons, we choose to treat symptoms with band-aids instead of treating the cause of the problem. Have we done away with tracking? Absolutely not, we simply hide it behind new course titles and curricula. Years ago in our schools, we had the workshop (skills) classes along with basic, standard and advanced placement (AP) classes. The terms "basic" and "standard" were obviously offensive to some, so now we have CP (college prep), honors, AP, and our school is a part of the International Baccalaureate program. Guess what? Students are still tracked by ability level regardless of the names you give the classes. The class titles have changed—along with inflated grade point levels—but the classes are comparable to what they were years ago, minus the inflated grade levels.

There will always be differences in the ability of students, some kids are going to work harder, and some kids are going to be smarter than others. The bottom line is that if we can raise all kids to where they can do their best, we will have achieved more than most thought possible. Do the right things, and good things will happen. Help create that moldable clay early on, give your teachers that clay and the support they need, and see what happens.

Chapter 5

Administration and the Peter Principle

JF:

One of the toughest things teachers have to deal with relates to inconsistencies in leadership at the school and district level. I realize that it is not easy being an administrator in the current educational environment, but continuity and consistency at the building level are imperative to gain the trust of faculty, staff and students. This takes individuals who have experience in the educational environment and know how things work and should work in a school. What I have observed in my years of teaching is a trend toward "career administrators." People that may spend a few years teaching but have a burning desire to move up the ladder. Teaching for three to five years is "teething" with regard to a teaching career. I thought I knew a bunch after teaching for five years, but after teaching for 30, I realize that I was nowhere near having the insight and forethought needed to be the best that I could be. Some of these young administrators don't have the foundation or appreciation of the challenges that teachers face in the classroom, and how to help teachers work through problems as opposed to some administrative "BS" about how to effectively operate a classroom. Teaching for them is a means to move up the career ladder into administration. The problem is that many of these people are poster children for "The Peter Principle" — people in bureaucracies that are promoted beyond their level of competence.

Just because one has a degree doesn't mean that he or she will be an effective school administrator. If young teachers become administrators too quickly, their inexperience can be disastrous for a school.

For several years, I observed a trend in our system where a former superintendent liked to play "musical chairs" with principals during summer breaks. This appeared to me to be an attempt to break up traditional loyalties and perceived "power" networks in favor of the central administration having the only consistency in the system. This "educational leader" wanted "building managers," not principals. It was the central administration that would dictate policy, regardless of whether it was beneficial for a school and its community. From talking to other teachers, this may be a trend in many states. In my opinion, this upheaval is detrimental to the morale of faculties and staff in these individual schools. After 10 principals in 30 years, I feel that consistency of leadership is crucial to the overall "health" of a school. The teachers, staff and students know what to expect and how to work within the various parameters of leadership styles. Schools need consistent leadership in order to function effectively.

Leadership Styles Are Different

There are many leadership styles used in school systems, some much more effective than others. There is the authoritarian model, where the administrators try to rule with an iron fist, intimidation is the rule of thumb, and people are publicly chastised and humiliated—sometimes in front of a classroom full of students. The last time I checked, we were in the people business. This is no way to treat teachers, staff or students—although for some it may seem to be the easiest way to rule. These people never last too long, and they leave a "scorched earth" of morale in their wake. Combine this "leadership" style with subjective performance evaluations of teachers and staff, and it is easy to understand how this can exacerbate tension between administration and school staff. Over the past few years, the "team" approach seems to be the "paradigm of the month" with leadership teams and administrative teams that give the impression of site-based or collective leadership at the school level. This is all well and good, until the team approach breaks down with an administrative decree that robs trust from faculty and staff. I personally prefer the authoritative approach, where the leader demonstrates a firm, fair approach with a nurturing outlook for those that work in the school environment that they are responsible for. This approach builds trust among those that make up the school—from teachers and staff, to students and parents. Principals must be strong, effective leaders because they are ultimately responsible for what goes on in the school. It's the style of what they say and how they implement their decisions that ultimately determines how effective their leadership can be. The administrator that is seen to care for the well being of the students, faculty and staff will command the loyalty and support of those within the school and in the school community. I have seen all three of these styles over my years in education, and I have seen our school climate go up and down like a rollercoaster too many times.

HA:

What Makes an Effective School Principal?

Matthew Clifford, senior research scientist at the American Institutes of Research (AIR), and Steven Ross, professor of education at John Hopkins University's Center for Research and Reform in Education, said, "Despite the potential for successful principal evaluations to improve schools, improvements in principal evaluations systems are 'long overdue'" (*eSchool News*, September 2011). Raishay Lin, a contributing editor of *eSchool News*, writes:

> Research suggests that good principals can create dramatic improvement in K–12 schools, particularly in the lowest performing schools—but the consistency, fairness, and value of current principal evaluation practices remain questionable.

The National Association of Elementary School Principals (NAESP) provided guidance to improve evaluations of principals. The research emphasizes the effect that principals have on:

- school culture
- teacher quality and satisfaction
- policy implementation

However, according to Clifford, the research also reveals that there's a lot of accountability without the recognition that people need to develop. Clifford said:

> Constructive evaluation to help principals improve is key in light of federal policies such as School Improvement Grants that replace principals deemed ineffective (*eSchool News*, September 2011).

Clifford notes that good evaluations for principals should address four areas of a principal's performance such as:

- effectiveness as a curriculum and instructional leader
- school climate factors such as teacher working conditions and parent attitudes
- student achievement and observation
- data
- how a principal manages teacher meetings

Clifford and Ross, through NAESP guidelines, "will expedite the redesign principal evaluations systems nationwide" (*eSchool News*, September 2011).

JF:

Support Personnel Are Important

I know that I have mentioned staff in speaking about the school environment and what I am talking about is the support personnel. The custodians, cafeteria workers, secretaries and teacher's assistants need to feel that they are an integral part of the school. All too often, people speak of the faculty and neglect to consider the needs of the support personnel. We should appreciate the work done by our support staff and demonstrate to them that they play an important role in the success of the school. We are all in this together, and when we acknowledge that and work together, our schools will be better. A positive working environment for all involved contributes to the overall school climate that is observed by all those involved in the school community.

HA:

Support Staff Appreciate the Efforts of Their President

As observers of the efforts of Joe and Tiffany Franks' determination to provide their support staff with special recognition can see, much was ventured and accomplished. Dr. Tiffany Franks, President of Averett University in Danville, Virginia, and her husband, Joe Franks, recognized a need and fulfilled it as never before. They have opened their home to every group employed at the university for many social and special events at Averett. As a result, those employees feel a real part of the university and are very loyal to Joe and Tiffany as well as the university.

Leaders Are Made, Not Born

For years, people have disagreed over the question of whether leaders are born to lead or whether people can be trained to be leaders. Warren Bennis, a national expert on leadership and author of several books on leadership, joins experts in the field of leadership insisting that leaders are made, not born. "If the basic desire to learn to lead exists, the major capacities and competencies of leadership can be learned" (Bennis and Namus 1997). Bennis and Namus write that many people are convinced that leaders are born, not made, summoned in to their calling through some unfathomable process. Those of the right breed could lead, all others must be led. No amount of learning or yearning could change your fate (Bennis and Namus 1997). They reason that nurture is more important than nature in determining who becomes a successful leader. They comment that: It will no longer be enough for leaders to issue pious platitudes about innovation while they eviscerate their research departments. Slogans of the week just won't get it. Leaders will have to be architects and cheerleaders for change. Bennis and Namus conclude that the sport administrator in the new century will have the opportunity to fill the leadership void by drawing people to them and leading people to places they have not been before (Bennis and Namus 1997). David P. Campbell, an expert on leadership, developed the Campbell Leadership Index (CLI). Campbell, a member of the staff of the Center for Creative Leadership, defines leadership as "actions which focus resources to create desirable opportunities" (Campbell 1991). Campbell describes actions of leadership as "planning, organizing, managing, deciding, speaking, writing, producing, cajoling, motivating, creating, economizing, inspiring, disciplining, politicking, persuading, compromising, confronting, perhaps even litigating." Resources are defined as "people, money, time, space, and materials but also nebulous assets such as public opinion, legislative power, unique talents, opportunistic accidents (for instance, disasters that can be turned to some useful end), geographic disadvantages, and personal contacts." A powerful example is the leadership furnished to not only New Yorkers but the entire world by New York Mayor Rudy Guliani during the September 11, 2001 terrorist attack. Guliani truly accepted the challenge and became a leader as never before. Campbell specifies that there are seven tasks that must be achieved if leadership is to occur. They include "vision, management, empowerment, politics, feedback, entrepreneurship, and personal style." Regarding one of the tasks, personal style, Campbell emphasizes: The leader is the most visible individual in the organization and, consequently, everyone else. If the leader is competent, optimistic, and trustworthy, a positive spirit will usually pervade the organization. If, in contrast, the leader is incompetent, meanspirited, or unethical, a less productive atmosphere will likely result. Authorities on leadership such as Campbell and Bennis stress the importance of developing leaders rather than managers and set a high standard for the modern sports administrator to attain. David Scott, assistant professor of sport administration at the University of New Mexico, concurs with Billick and other authorities on leadership and their comments that there are a number of definitions of leadership. Scott believes that leadership involves "vision and the ability to influence or motivate people toward goal attainment." He writes that leadership "provides direction and support. Leadership creates change and is rooted in principles, morality, and ethics" (*Successful Sport Management* 2000). Scott has his list of traits and suggests that leaders have special abilities such as:

- ability to obtain the trust and respect of individuals and groups;
- ability to adapt to various situations or contingencies;
- ability to develop vision and clarify a path;
- motivation and inspiration of followers;
- ability to achieve results (*Successful Sport Management* 2000).

The Center For Creative Leadership, in Greensboro, North Carolina, described leadership when it said, "The highest predictor of success in an organization is leadership that functions with integrity and honesty ... Other core traits are trustworthiness, loyalty and pride" (Billick 2001). In my experience in administration, I have observed certain characteristics and qualities of leadership in other administrators. Outstanding leaders possess most of the following nine characteristics.

1. The ability to relate to people—Getting along with people is absolutely essential for success. Sports administration is truly a people industry, and sports administrators who avoid people are in the wrong profession. Research reveals that more administrators lose their jobs not from a lack of knowledge of the industry, but from their inability to get along with people.

2. A sense of caring—For years I asked student-athletes to describe a sports administrator who they felt stood out favorably in their minds. Without exception every group described a leader that touched their lives as someone who cared about them. Genuine caring can never be disguised and students from nursery to grad-

uate school cannot be fooled. Caring means respecting the self-worth and dignity of a person.

3. A sense of humor — I find that a sense of humor, the ability to laugh and not take oneself too seriously, is one of the most important qualities of an athletics director.

4. Self-discipline — I was coaching football at Chowan Junior College in eastern North Carolina. On the first day of football practice, I was disappointed with the physical condition of the squad. I received a telephone call from Earle Edwards, head coach of the N.C. State Wolfpack, inviting our team to a post-season game against his talented freshman team. I declined, telling him we would not be a match for his outstanding players. I relayed my conversation to the team, and their reaction was immediate: call back and agree that you will check with him later in the season before you turn it down. I said I wanted them to be in top condition by practicing self-discipline — stopping any cigarette smoking and drinking, and keeping good hours. Several weeks later, the co-captains reported that all but three men had stopped smoking. A week later the captains reported that 100 percent were observing all training rules. Through self-discipline, the team had the first undefeated season in school history, and true to our agreement, we played the N.C. State freshmen on Thanksgiving Day.

5. Accepting responsibility — It is easy to talk about responsibility, but accepting it is often a different story. When I look for leadership in any group, I look for people who are willing to accept responsibility and carry it out.

6. The ability to make decisions — This characteristic is so important that it separates the outstanding from the average sport administrator. President Harry Truman, one of my favorite leaders, made famous the phrases, "The buck stops here" and "If you can't stand the heat, get out of the kitchen." When historians judge our past presidents, they use a certain guide: In a time of crisis, did he have the ability to make decisions? Certainly Truman did with his controversial decision to use the atomic bomb and the firing of General Douglas MacArthur. During my years as a sport administrator, I worked with many who had different leadership styles. When I teach sports administration courses, I require the students

to read *The Achiever* in which Gerald Bell discusses six leadership styles: commander, attacker, avoider, pleaser, performer and achiever (Bell 1973). Students aspiring to leadership roles in sports particularly appreciate the book. Most administrators I know are mixtures of the six characteristics, but the successful ones have the ability to make decisions. I find that coaches may not always agree with the decisions of an administrator, but they admire the person who can and will make a decision. Tom Butters, former athletics director at Duke University, described a situation that reveals the type of job a sport administrator holds. A security man approached him just as Duke was about to start the NCAA's Final Four basketball game against Kentucky, informing him that a threat had just been made against the life of starting forward Gene Banks. Butters had literally seconds to make a difficult decision. He made it and agreed to let the game be played. Minutes later a member of the Iron Dukes Booster Club tapped him on the shoulder clutching a hot dog and said, "This is the last damn time I'm going to stand for these cold hot dogs." Butters said, "This is what's great about the job. There can be a crisis in the morning and something absurd in the afternoon" (*News & Record*, June 3, 1984). Butters made an unpopular decision when Mike Krzyzewski had a losing record in his first years at Duke. Butters refused to give in to the demands of unhappy alumni and other groups pressing for a change in coaches. No one doubts the wisdom of Butters today as Coach "K" is recognized as one of the top, if not the best, college coaches in the United States. If Butters had not possessed the foresight to recognize genuine quality and talent in his coach, Duke would have been the loser. Dante in *The Inferno* said it best, "The hottest fires in Hell are reserved for those who in time of moral crisis maintain their neutrality."

7. Courage—When I was a junior in college, I received a call from the local high school asking me to officiate a football game that afternoon. The teams were bitter rivals, and the game had barely started when I made my first mistake. I turned to a man who called me an SOB and said that I would meet him after the game. Without hesitation he said, "You're on." What a foolish thing for me to do, but as a 20-year-old college student, you often react when you should think and use good judgment. After the game, the vis-

iting fans, convinced that I caused the loss, surrounded me, ready to fight. I could find no friendly face in the crowd when suddenly a familiar face appeared, a fraternity brother elbowing his way toward me. To my surprise, he turned to the man facing me and said, "Herb is my friend, and no one except this person in front of him better tangle with him. If anyone does, he will deal with me." There was something in his voice that commanded respect and, unbelievable but true, everyone in the crowd left without a word spoken. I later learned that my friend had been a Navy Ace in the Pacific Theatre in World War II. From that day on, I realized what one person, willing to stand alone, could do. Monk Critcher, the Navy Ace, influenced my life and gave me the inspiration to speak out on unpopular issues even if it meant standing alone. On my desk is a plaque that quotes President Andrew Jackson: "One person with courage makes a majority." By the nature of the job, sports administrators will continue to face challenges almost daily—courage to stand alone can be one of the finest attributes of leadership.

8. The ability to empower others—Upon retirement, a chief executive officer of a prominent national corporation was asked what he would do differently if he started over. He replied that he lacked the ability or willingness to delegate duties because he thought that no one could do the job but him. In my opinion, the ability to empower others to assist you in your work is the effective use of leadership skills. I witnessed the good work empowerment accomplished on our staff. Many of our alumni coaches had outstanding coaching records in football with Top 10 teams in the states of Virginia, North Carolina, and South Carolina. For some reason we were not getting our quota of the alumni coaches' players. I knew they loved the college and the football program but something was definitely wrong. When I raised the question the answers were all the same, your present coaches do not seem to want our student-athletes. On the other hand, the coaches said they did not have the scholarship money other schools had to recruit the blue-chip players. I asked the coaches to consider an annual alumni football clinic on campus with alumni coaches serving as clinicians. This would be a great public relations venture between alumni coaches and staff. An assistant coach loved the idea and volunteered to run the entire op-

eration. The head coach was reluctant to empower the assistant coach but finally gave him the authority. The alumni clinic became so successful that major universities would call to check the dates of our clinic so their clinics would not conflict with ours. The alumni clinics accomplished more than I ever hoped, with the assistant receiving attention from coaches and college officials who recognized his outstanding work. I am certain it led to his advancement as head coach at a very fine institution. In the process of empowerment, athletics directors need to make individuals feel that they can make a difference. It has been said that empowerment enables administrators to somehow encourage ordinary people to do the work of superior people. Bennis, in his book, *Why Leaders Can't Lead*, writes that in leadership, empowerment of others is more important than power (Bennis 1989).

9. Values—This may be the most important trait of all for leaders. Leaders who have the confidence of others have a sense of loyalty, integrity, honesty and trustworthiness. During my years in sports, leaders with these qualities gained the respect of their workers, students, athletes and others who were working for role models. On loyalty, Maurice Franks, associate professor at Southern University Law Center, wrote that "loyalty cannot be blueprinted. It cannot be produced on an assembly line. In fact, it cannot be manufactured at all, for the organ is the human heart, the center of self-respect and human dignity" (Billick 2001). An administrator at a small college recently admitted that, in many instances, loyalty is a quality that is being eliminated in our society. He said that while many people are extremely loyal to their employers, the employer is no longer loyal to the employee. Unfortunately the observation by the administrator is too often the case. An illustration of devoted loyalty happened when the Boston Celtics were playing the Houston Rockets for the NBA Championship. Our basketball coach hurried home to hear the pregame radio interview in the hope that the announcer might interview M.L. Carr, an All-American on the 1973 Guilford College national champions. The telephone rang and our coach reluctantly answered, preferring to listen to the radio and possibly hearing the voice of M.L. Carr. The voice on the line surprised our coach who asked, "How can you be

calling when you are on TV warming up for the game?" Carr explained the network had set up the radio line and he asked if he could make a quick call to his college coach. "I just wanted you to know that I'm thinking of you tonight and the championship we won in Kansas City." The Celtics went out that night and won the championship. For M.L. Carr, the Celtic victory was important, but so was the NAIA National Championship won by Guilford College in 1973. Today, M.L. Carr is a successful businessman in Alabama and is a trustee at Guilford College. He is an example of a person who exhibited and continues to be loyal to his alma mater. David Scott summarizes the importance of leadership for the new century sport administrator when he writes: The leaders of the future will not only need to provide insightful direction, they will need to be actively engaged as facilitators and supports. Ultimately sport leaders for the new millenium must radiate optimism and facilitate solutions that enhance the role of sport in society and satisfactorily address the diverse needs of employees, participants, and customers within this great industry (Appenzeller and Lewis 2000).

Fail-Safe Leadership

Linda Martin and Dr. David Mutchler, in a text that is not a typical book on leadership (*Fail-Safe Leadership* 2001), quote retired Army Colonel Dandridge Malone: "The very essence of leadership is its purposes. And the purpose of leadership is to accomplish a task. That is what leadership does — and what it does is more important than what it is and how it works." James B. Godshall, President of Total Quality Institute, writes that there is "an overabundance of managers and a huge lack of leaders." He describes leaders as people who: Come in different ages, genders, roles, profiles, nationalities, behavioral styles, etc. There really is no prototype for a leader, which explains why so many attempts at leadership training continue to fail (*Fail-Safe Leadership* 2001). It is obvious from lists of leadership styles advocated by so many authors who describe the characteristics of leaders that Martin and Mutchler believe that leaders get results. This is the basis of their book on leadership — leaders get results! They believe that whatever characteristics of leaders are used, the main purpose is to get results. This is a novel and innovative approach to leadership and one that should be explored by those interested in leadership.

Global Leadership Deficit

Thomas Friedman, a columnist for the *New York Times*, asked the question, "Any leaders, among the wired hordes of followers?" Friedman wrote that in all of his travels, he gets the same question whether it is in Europe as well as the United States:

> Why does it feel like so few leaders are capable of inspiring their people to meet the challenges of our day?

Friedman attempts to answer his own question when he says:

> Watching European, Arab and U.S. leaders grappling with their respective crises... the quality of political leadership declines with every 100 million new users of Facebook and Twitter.

He explains that:

> The wiring of the world through social media and web-enabled cell phones is changing the nature of conversations between leaders and the led everywhere.... Leaders are listening to so many voices all the time that they become prisoners of them ... *(News & Record*, June 26, 2012).

Friedman believes social media has a detrimental effect on those who should be leaders, not followers. He calls it the "uber-ideology of our day," and defines it as popularism that leads to the following:

> Read the polls, track the blogs, tally the Twitter feeds and Facebook postings, and go precisely where the people are, not where they need to go.

This prompts the question, "If everyone is following, who is leading?" Friedman believes leaders face challenges to ask people to share burdens, not benefits. Leaders, he says, need to tell the truth — that "requires extraordinary leadership."

Friedman's article goes on to quote Dov Seidman, whose company LRN advises CEOs that "Nothing inspires people more than the truth." Friedman further makes his point when he writes, "Most leaders think that telling people the truth makes that leader vulnerable — either to the public or their opponents. They are wrong." The article concludes with Seidman's point that

> The most important part of telling the truth is that it bonds you to people, because when you trust people with the truth, they trust you back. Trusting people with the truth is like giving them a solid floor. When you are anchored in shared truth, you start to share problems together.

Friedman adds:

> This is not what we are getting from leaders in America, the Arab world or Europe... Whichever leader does that can enlist people in the truth will have real followers and friends not the virtual ones (*News & Record*, June 26, 2012).

School administrators, principals and teachers alike can profit from the recommendations of Friedman and Seidman. *Leadership starts at the top!*

The Peter Principle: Know It, See It, Avoid It!

Joyce Richman, a career counselor and author, whose book *Road, Routes, and Ruts: A Guidebook for Career Success* is widely read by people seeking employment, wrote about the Peter Principle. She discussed the *Peter Principle* by Dr. Laurence J. Peter and Raymond Hill and described it as "A belief that organizations promote competent people until they are no longer competent" (*News & Record*, Nov. 25, 2012).

Richman describes a man she calls Jack (not his real name). "Jack was the operations manager who was so great at trouble-shooting and problem solving, he was promoted to manager of strategic planning ... It took about six months for Jack to go from 'what a guy' to 'what's with this guy.'" Richman analyzed Jack's problem and described it as follows:

> Everything that Jack had done to become successful in his prior role had no relevance in his new role. Hands-on-Jack didn't know how to be a hands-on-manager. He didn't know how to lead because he didn't know where he was supposed to go.

His goals were clear in his previous position, his expectations defined. "Jack understood what his previous boss wanted, and he delivered." Jack did "all his work on the ground, one tree at a time." When Jack used "his old tactic to the new job, he came across as a micromanager. The more he crowded his workers, the more they resisted, until they gave in, gave up, or got out."

The sad thing about Jack was that "he was outgoing, resourceful, creative, responsive and goal focused." He was none of these in his new job. He retreated from his job, lost confidence, hesitated in his responses and second-guessed himself. Unfortunately, Jack was moved from competence to incompetence. According to Richman, that is the *Peter Principle*! She recommends that:

> If it's your job to identify which talent to promote to what role, you'll want to evaluate which competencies are applicable to what positions. You'll want to separate strengths (what is innate) from skills (what is learned).

Richman gives good advice regarding the Peter Principle when she writes:

> Once you've determined which employees are ready, assign them tests projects. Watch what they do and how they do it, what they move toward and do best and what they delay and do least well. Coach and provide them outgoing feedback that is supportive and constructive.

As suspected, I witnessed many outstanding people with various competencies be promoted to various positions in which they failed miserably. I saw several examples of outstanding teachers (professors) who were great mentors, super researchers who were promoted to positions of deans. One was extremely popular with his students, well-respected by the faculty and staff, but a failure as a dean. Another outstanding professor was promoted to Alumni Director but did not stand accountable for the rigors of the job. Unfortunately he was terminated and left the teaching profession as well as other related positions. As Richmond wrote, "know it, see it, and avoid it" (*News & Record*, Nov. 25, 2012).

Chapter 6

Welcome to My Paradigm

JF:

Alice Cooper once had a song called, "Welcome to My Nightmare." For years, I would dread the start of a new school year, because invariably it would begin with a new focus—or experiment, as I would call it. Previously, I mentioned the "paradigm of the month" with regard to administrative leadership. This phrase can easily be used to describe the educational curricula that "come down from on high" to help lead us to the promised land of student achievement. Teaching is inundated with new "buzzwords" and methods that are touted as being the best to maximize achievement. While some may be wonderful and useful, unless there is a clear long-term commitment to them by central administration, they may serve to confuse and frustrate those they are supposed to help—students and teachers. All too often, these innovative ideas are around for a couple of years, then replaced with a "new and improved" method. Let me give you an example from my system. A few years ago, the "buzz" in our system dealt with the "Paideia" method of teaching. Paideia is an interesting theoretical concept where discussion and dialogue would enhance learning through student involvement, interaction and reflection. There are many school systems that have embraced this and I'm sure some of them have experienced a great deal of success. Unfortunately, in my system this was not the case. Members of our faculty went to be trained in this new method and learn how to facilitate student learning in their classrooms. On the surface, this was intriguing and in training sessions where we had small group interaction it worked well. The problem was that a class of 33 students does not comprise a small group. When asked about this, we were given some alternative responsibilities for students not directly involved in the small group discussions. For example, students not directly involved were to be "observers" of what was happening in the "Paideia process." They were to take notes from their observations to share with the group at a later stage in the evaluation process. The bottom line is that the Paideia method was designed for small group interaction, and most classes in our public schools were too big to be used effectively. In addition, while the intention was to be cross-curricular, it was difficult to implement this strategy in certain classes. I know of an administrator who, in trying to make a point with a teacher, actually made a weight lifting class sit in a circle on the gym floor to reflect on how weight training could help them be better human beings—give me a break. Why not just hold hands and sing "kumbaya"?

If common sense was applied to how we try to implement these educational strategies, they would be much more effective and well received by teachers and students. There is no doubt that this technique could be very effective if it were given the proper environment. And it is no secret that smaller class sizes have a direct impact on student learning and achievement—but this involves a commitment to dedicate the necessary funds to facilitate smaller class sizes. That type of long-term financial commitment is rarely seen in public education. Nevertheless, Paideia faded into the background for the majority of us, to be eventually replaced with something new—like "minute by minute" classroom assessment strategies. That's what I dealt with in my 30th year to rock the student achievement world.

If you need a smile, check out the "Make it Official" document of bureaucratic buzzwords and see if you recognize some phrases that have been thrown at you in teachers meetings or educational workshops. I was given this by a colleague over 25 years ago as one of those Xeroxed joke sheets that people used to give each other before email. I must confess that I have used some of these over the years to detour some overzealous administrators and they never said a word asking me to explain! And of course, Herb and I thought about using it to create the title to this book, then we smiled and decided to stick with the original idea.

MAKE IT OFFICIAL

COLUMN ONE	COLUMN TWO	COLUMN THREE
0. INTEGRATED	0. MANAGEMENT	0. OPTIONS
1. TOTAL	1. ORGANIZATIONAL	1. FLEXIBILITY
2. SYSTEMIZED	2. MONITORED	2. CAPABILITY
3. PARALLEL	3. RECIPROCAL	3. MOBILITY
4. FUNCTIONAL	4. DIGITAL	4. PROGRAMMING
5. RESPONSIVE	5. LOGISTICAL	5. CONCEPT
6. OPTIONAL	6. TRANSITIONAL	6. TIME-PHASE
7. SYNCHRONIZED	7. INCREMENTAL	7. PROJECTION
8. COMPATIBLE	8. THIRD-GENERATION	8. HARDWARE
9. BALANCE	9. POLICY	9. CONTINGENCY

Think of any three-digit number, then select the corresponding buzzword from the above three columns. For instance, 582 produces "responsive third-generation capability," a phrase that can be dropped into virtually any report or speech with that ring of decisive, knowledgeable authority. No one will have the remotest idea of what you are talking about, but the important thing is that they're not about to admit it.

MUDDLE IT LIKE A BUREAUCRAT

Chapter 7

"A" for Accountability

JF:

In today's educational environment, taxpayers and politicians want to get the biggest bang for their buck with regard to how schools are performing. They demand accountability for student achievement. Thus, we have entered the era of standardized testing. And why not? It is a measurable, objective and easy way to evaluate the performance of students. The problem is that we have put the accountability portion of education on the backs of teachers and schools with very little on the student. If the student doesn't achieve to desired levels or does not meet some arbitrary measure of "growth," it is the teacher's fault—the teachers are obviously not doing their job. And if the overall scores are not high enough, the administrators are not doing their job. As this has evolved, school administrators have become obsessed and paranoid about test scores, and this is transferred to create a pressure cooker in many schools. Not a great educational environment by any means. Simply look at the scandal in Atlanta, Georgia, in 2011 where test security was compromised and some school personnel were reviewing with students what was actually on the standardized examination. In addition, a culture of "teaching to the test" has emerged where we are producing "cookie cutter" teachers who are groomed to teach the same way, given standardized district "pacing guides" so every teacher is basically teaching the same thing at the same time, and utilizing test banks created by bureaucrats to prepare students to achieve on these standardized tests. What I have observed is that we are losing the creative element that helps teachers love this profession and students love to be in a classroom. In my opinion, this creates disenchantment and is another contributing factor of people leaving the profession. Yet this is merely a reflection of how this society deals with challenges where there are no easy solutions. It has become our nature to find the easiest and/or quickest solution to the problem, not necessarily the best. We take the lowest bids in construction, with little concern about getting real quality materials or workmanship. As anyone knows, you get what you pay for and that maintenance costs over the long term may increase the real cost of a project many fold. The unintended consequences of the "low bid" process are evident in every community in our country. I teach in a school whose main building was constructed in 1929 and the classroom doors in this building are still functional. Contrast that with new construction that took place in 1999 in which the door handles lasted about one year and the school system has had to drill spots to create makeshift handles to allow the doors to be functional.

See the Forest AND the Trees

In our society, too often we look for a simple solutions when it may not be the most efficient or equitable. Case in point — Affirmative Action. This program, designed to increase access and opportunity to those once denied it, was laudable and intended to help groups of people who had been historically discriminated against. It was never intended to be intentionally discriminatory to another group, for people to accuse it of "reverse discrimination." It was never intentioned to create some type of quota system, but that was the easiest way to accommodate the provisions of the policy. Thus it came under fire and there was a backlash against it. Standardized testing may not be the best way to evaluate student achievement, but until a better way is found, we have to deal with it. Can we make it better and more efficient? I believe that we can. If minimum standards are established for the public educational system and students are held accountable to achieving minimum competencies from day one in the public schools, we can begin to eliminate many of the pitfalls of public education. Minimum standards need to be established, students need to meet them, and we need to have politicians and educational bureaucrats with the backbone to see that these standards are achieved prior to promotion. Please don't give me the argument that the child's self-esteem will suffer irreparable damage if they are held back. We can learn from failure. When we prop students up and prevent setbacks, what are we teaching them about life beyond school, when their boss really isn't concerned about their self esteem—she or he wants results. What does it do for a high school senior's self-esteem when they read at below a fifth grade level because they were socially promoted? We MUST have students achieve minimum competencies before they are promoted, and must provide the environment that ensures the achievement of these competencies. If that means alternative educational programs and schools, so be it. Do I mean the possibility of separate schools for remediation, discipline and adjustment issues? Yes I do. In such schools the resources can be used to provide the extra counseling, supervision, smaller class sizes and attention to give struggling students a decent chance. How are we going to pay for this? By making hard choices. Only in this way can the concept of a real "No Child Left Behind" become a reality. This idea may not be politically correct, but it is necessary. As long as we have standardized testing, we need to ensure that items being tested at the public school level represent the basic competencies and knowledge base that will help young people be successful beyond their public school years. Practicality and level appropriateness should be the rule of thumb in these tests. I recall hearing one of my colleagues remark that a certain Level I End of Course Test in math was so difficult that they would be amazed if any kid finished it. What purpose does that serve? When we establish basic competencies and students are held accountable, the test should simply reinforce that those concepts are mastered. If we can create tests that demonstrate how students have a comprehension of the "big picture" cause and effect, as opposed to obscure facts we will achieve more long term success. We need for students to see the forest, and the trees. For example, if we have a test in Civics, why not ensure that the students could answer questions that are used on citizenship examinations? On that line, we need to have administrators who can see the trees! Some administrators may have great ideas for the big picture, but not be able to implement policies in efficient ways to get their school or their system to that point. We need people who understand and care about the issues that teachers face every day in their classrooms and do everything in their power to ensure that teachers have the opportunity to do their job. In my opinion, the key characteristic of an effective administrator is empathy. When I talk to someone who can tell me how they understand what I am going through, that helps us work together to help me be better and help the students that I work with. And unless they have been there, and have the foundation of teaching experience, they may never become a truly effective administrator. In addition, I believe that every administrator, from the building level to the superintendent, should have to substitute teach for one day each month across the realm of schools in their system—let them experience what we deal with each and every day!

HA:

Hold Everyone Accountable

Joe Franks is on target when he advocates holding everyone connected with teaching accountable. With the release of the New Teacher Project report, the National Education Association (NEA) agrees that "attracting and retaining great teachers must be a top priority. And it will only become more urgent over the next decade, when we will need 1.6 million new teachers, according to the U.S. Department of Education." Betsy Pringle, secretary/treasurer of NEA talks about such a challenge when she urges everyone to work together and "Hold everyone accountable for the success of our children." She also includes "Not only educators but principals, parents and the public officials who provide resources" (*USA Today*, August 8, 2012).

(JF: What about holding STUDENTS accountable?? This is part of the problem—too many experts holding everyone accountable

EXCEPT students, which may be the most important aspect of accountability!)

Pringle believes that states such as Massachusetts are setting higher standards of professional practice through a "Peer Assistance and Review Program." "Teachers and union and school districts have found common ground on tenure and performance, an approach that puts the needs of students first."

According to Pringle, we need to raise the quality of preparation long before they enter the classroom. She feels "that teacher evaluations must be meaningfully multifaceted and fair and involve teachers throughout their careers." She concludes:

> Teachers should share a leadership and partnership role with principals, administrators and policymakers ... attracting and retaining great teachers is one of the most important challenges we face. We can do it if we work together and put the needs of the students first (*USA Today*, August 8, 2012).

New Trends in Teacher Evaluation

In an attempt to improve evaluation of teachers, many schools are using a technique that emphasizes student involvement rather than teacher to teacher evaluation. The method corresponds to doctors in a teaching hospital using facts rather than value judgments. The method is called "instructional rounds" and "it looks at how well students are learning, rather than how well the teacher teaches."

Many schools evaluate teachers by going into the classroom while the new approach is just the opposite. The evaluators think of three things in their evaluation process:

1. Network—a group of educators who form a community over time
2. Classroom observations
3. Strategy, in the form of improvement plans

One characteristic of the new plan is "teams evaluate groups of classes at a school at one time." The group looks for trends at the school. "They focus on teaching and how it is received, instead of individual teacher performance." The article on "instructional rounds" concludes "This is not something we do to teachers. This is something we do with teachers" (*eSchool News*, July/August 2011).

States Strengthen Teacher Evaluation

In 2009, "only four states used student achievement as a predeterminance influence in how teacher performance is addressed." Today, according to a report from the National Council on Teacher Quality, "states count student teaching and 19 states and the District of Columbia use it as a criteria for firing teachers" (*eSchool News*, January 2012).

The American Federation of Teachers (AFT) want teacher evaluations conducted on the local level with teacher input and test scores kept to a limited basis. At a conference in July 2012, the National Education Association (NEA) delegates voted to "overhaul teacher evaluations." Most states use their evaluations to decide "pay, tenure, firings and the awarding of teaching licenses."

A Personal Experience on Evaluations

During my years at Guilford College, I was amazed at the faculty's negative reaction to their evaluations. During a heated discussion at a faculty meeting, the professors were emphatically told that the evaluations would positively have no effect on their retention, pay, tenure, etc. The majority's response was that the faculty did not believe this would be true. That year I was on the powerful Retention Committee and learned first hand that the student evaluations were used to determine promotion, tenure, firings and the awarding of endowed professorships. So much for the broken promises, which led to faculty distrust of the administrators.

Evaluate Us as Administrators

Only once during my 37 years on the faculty and administrative staff, did our president, academic dean and other administrators boldly tell the faculty that they wanted to be evaluated by the faculty and staff. The administrators said they welcomed the opportunity to have peer evaluation.

I and others believed it was to encourage faculty to accept the evaluation process. The faculty approved the effort on behalf of the administrators. When the evaluations were published, the administrators received such low ratings and so many negatives on their performance, ADMINISTRATORS NEVER AGAIN AGREED TO BE EVALUATED.

Posting Teacher Ratings Debated

In January, 2012, Meris Stansbury, an Associate Editor of *eSchool News*, commented on a controversial issue of publishing online teachers' ratings for all to see. Advocates believe society looks at ratings in practically every area of life—doctors in some states, movies, restaurants, etc. Why not teacher performance? The Center for American Progress (CAP) reported that the *Los Angeles Times* published the performance ratings for the Los Angeles Unified School District's teachers. Parents and the public "could look up specific teachers in the newspaper database and see how they ranked in math and English, from least effective to most effective in the District."

Teachers feel that there are so many factors besides standardized test scores to reflect the effectiveness of teachers. One issue is the morale factor. One Los Angeles teacher had a high rating for his dedication to his students and high rating by his peers, but was rated "less effective than average." Because of his low rating, available to parents and public, the teacher took his own life. If teachers are ranked publicly, public school teachers would be less willing to engage in the implementation of a new evaluation system.

It will be interesting to follow innovative programs that might implement a policy of ratings of teachers on an open scale. It is important for teachers to be involved in the evaluation program.

Once-a-Year Teacher Evaluations Are Not Enough

We have included several suggestions for the all-important topic of teacher evaluations. A Bill and Melinda Gates Foundation report found that once-a-year evaluation of teachers is not enough. According to the second part of the report, "School districts using infrequent classroom observations to decide who are their best—and their worst—teachers could be making some big mistakes."

The report, based on nationwide experiments of thousands of teachers concluded:

> Good teacher evaluations require multiple nuanced observations by trained evaluators. These results should be combined with other measures, such as student test scores and classroom surveys, together enough information to both evaluate teachers and help them improve.

The Gates report describes that the present type of evaluation consists, in too many instances, of "a single classroom observation every few years." Researchers say that this type of evaluative criteria has only 33 percent of any success as an evaluation technique.

Randi Weingarten, president of the American Federal of Teachers, believes that "there is too much emphasis being placed on evaluating teachers and not on improving their performance." Weingarten observes that:

Until we make a commitment to develop evaluation systems that are first and foremost about continuous improvement and professional growth, we will continue to struggle in our efforts to provide every child with a high quality education.

The core of the Gates report was to collect 13,000 digital videos of classroom teachers who volunteered to be studied. The report concluded:

- High quality classroom observations require clear, specific standards, well-trained and certified evaluators and multiple observations per teacher.
- Classroom evaluation is not enough. That information should be combined with student feedback and data on improvement in student test scores. Combining the three kinds of evaluations offset the weaknesses of each individual approach.

The different evaluation methods will need to be refined but they're better than what most school districts are using now (*eSchool News*, February 2012).

Effective Evaluations

What makes an effective school principal? Matthew Clifford, senior research scientist at the American Institute of Research and Stephen Ross, professor of education at Johns Hopkins University Center for Research and Reforming Education, said that despite the potential for successful principal evaluations to improve schools, improvements in principal evaluations are long overdue (*eSchool News*, September 2011). Raishay Lin, a contributing editor, suggests that good principals can create dramatic improvement in K–12 schools.

Chapter 8

The Hazing Dilemma

HA:

In the Sixth century AD, Emperor Justinian of Byzantine outlawed the hazing of first-year law students. There is no mention of hazing in written records again until the Middle Ages. Scholars propose that the practice was successfully eradicated until university members found old documents of codified Roman Law detailing Justinian's decree. It was then that students of the Middle Ages document hazing practices of first year students. From then until the present there has been a continuing issue with hazing (Nuwer, 1999).

Hazing reportedly is rampant and has received too little attention from school officials. However, school administrators and athletic administrators are beginning to realize the emotional, psychological and physical effects on students who are victims of hazing. In many instances coaches often treat hazing as "boys and girls will be boys and girls." To combat the practice, administrators need to define hazing, develop guidelines regarding school-wide events and implement effective punishment in hazing incidents. As a result of all the injuries and interest in the status of hazing on many levels, we are pleased that Dr. Colleen McGlone, professor at Coastal Carolina University, a national and international authority on hazing, agreed to edit and provide material on hazing for our readers.

Defining Hazing

Hazing is a broad term that encompasses many activities, situations and actions that an individual must tolerate in order to become part of the group or team. When trying to construct a definition of hazing, one must consider many different viewpoints. The definition and meaning of hazing often varies from one person to another. For example, an individual who is performing an act of hazing may define the term very differently than the person being hazed. An administrator may perceive hazing and the various acts involved differently than a coach or parent. Furthermore, some individuals may only consider physical bodily acts as hazing, while others may include mental and sexual acts as hazing activities. The definitions of hazing become the central focus when administrators are put in a position to decide if hazing occurred or if the activity was a case of horseplay gone wrong. While hazing has been acknowledged for centuries, there is no universally accepted definition. This may be due to the many forms and the variety of ways in which initiations and rituals take place within different organizations. In 1999, the following definition of hazing was postulated by Hoover: "Any activity expected of someone joining a group that humiliates, degrades, abuses, or endangers, regardless of the person's willingness to participate." Hoover's definition brings to light one of the common myths associated with hazing. There is an underlying myth that if a person participates in an initiation ceremony voluntarily, the initiation process cannot be considered "hazing." Hoover's definition proposes that an activity that humiliates, degrades, abuses or endangers another is an act of hazing regardless of the individual's willingness to participate. In addition, several state laws dispute this myth, including Texas law which states, "It is not a defense to prosecution for the offense under this subchapter that the person against whom the hazing was directed consented to or acquiesced in the hazing activity" (Sec. 4.54). Moreover, these definitions provide a more detailed explanation of what hazing entails, making it easier for policy makers and athletic directors to effectively illustrate the activities that may be considered as hazing.

Types of Hazing

There are two distinct categories of hazing: physical and mental. The physical form of hazing may include activities such as beatings, branding, paddling, excessive exercises, excessive drinking and/or drug use, and forced sexual activities. In addition, activities involving sexual activities and/or sexual assaults are considered forms of physical hazing. Sexual hazing often includes simulated sex acts, sodomy and forced kissing. Mental hazing often goes overlooked or undetected, but is just as dangerous as physical hazing. Mental hazing occurs when an initiate feels that they are in a dangerous situation or that there is a high degree of embarrassment involved with the activity. Types of mental hazing may include verbal abuse, being blindfolded, and being captured and locked in small places (Nuwer, 2000). Another form of mental hazing includes simulating sexual activities. Mental and physical hazing can occur separately or in conjunction with one another based upon the activities and the perspective of the person being hazed.

Prevalence of Hazing

- Over 250,000 hazed on college athletic teams
- 100 percent of surveyed athletes were "involved in some sort of initiation"
- 1 in 5 were "subjected to unacceptable or potentially illegal hazing"
- 66 percent were subjected to hazing that involved humiliation tactics
- "Women were most likely to be involved in alcohol-related hazing"
- Athletes identified and acknowledged a wide variety of hazing type behaviors, but they were reluctant to label them "hazing"
- 16 percent of the female athletes were involved in activities that carried a high probability of risk or that could result in criminal charges (Hoover, 1999)

The Statistics

Hazing has been troublesome for centuries. However, it has only been in the last 10 years that this topic has been the focus of research. In 1999, Alfred University was the first to conduct a large scale hazing study after dealing with a hazing-related death on their campus. This landmark study provided the first empirical data showing how prevalent hazing was on college campuses across the country. The Alfred study established baseline figures for the prevalence and severity of hazing. As a result, many colleges and universities have established policies and procedures in an effort to reduce the number of hazing incidents within intercollegiate athletics. While society has recognized the issue of hazing in athletics, the prevalence and severity of the problem may not be fully known, nor understood.

Hazing Is Not Just an Athletic Issue!
Researchers Detail Initial Results of Landmark College Hazing Study

A new study by University of Maine researchers reveals that hazing is commonplace in all kinds of college student organizations, and that most students don't recognize that some forms of dangerous, even illegal, behavior constitute hazing. The survey, known as the "National Study on Hazing," is by far the largest and most comprehensive study of its kind. Part of a three year research project, it includes responses from 11,482 college students at 53 institutions around the U.S. A research advisory group helped define a list of forced behaviors that constitute hazing. A partial list includes:

- Attendance at a skit night or roast where team members are humiliated
- Wearing clothing that is embarrassing and not part of the uniform
- Being yelled, screamed or cursed at by other team/organization members
- Acting as a personal servant to other organization member

- Enduring harsh weather without proper clothing
- Drinking large amounts of a non-alcoholic beverage such as water
- Drinking large amounts of alcohol to the point of passing out or getting sick
- Watching live sex acts
- Performing sex acts with the same gender

The study notes that "Stereotypes often shape perceptions of hazing as only a problem for Greek-letter organizations and athletes, and hazing behaviors are often dismissed as simply harmless antics and pranks."

The survey also reveals that one-quarter of those who experienced hazing believe that coaches and/or advisers were aware of the activities. A similar percentage of respondents report that alumni were present when hazing occurred. In more than half the incidents reported by students, photos of the activities were posted on public Web sites and roughly 25 percent of students report that hazing occurred in public spaces on campus.

Legal Aspects

As the number of reported hazing incidents has increased, so has the number of states that have passed legislation to deter hazing from occurring. Currently, there are 44 states with anti-hazing statutes while six states have not developed or introduced anti-hazing laws. Only the states of Alaska, Hawaii, Montana, New Mexico, South Dakota and Wyoming lack any type of hazing law (Nuwer, 2008). In 1969, 35 states had laws regarding hazing, this was the last year no fraternity, sorority or athletic death occurred in the U.S. (Hazing.hanknuwer.com). Hazing is punishable under criminal law in 40 states. Since hazing is considered a criminal act, the judicial system has established many other legal definitions that address and define hazing. Current hazing legislation varies from state to state, and the punishments for hazing may include a fine, imprisonment or both depending on the state and the severity of the hazing incident. With the various definitions of hazing, the aver-

age individual may have great difficulty determining what consti-
tutes hazing, as well as what types of behaviors may be regarded
as hazing. Similarly, when one looks at the legal definitions of hazing and anti-hazing statutes, it becomes increasingly difficult to develop legislation that encompasses all aspects of hazing without
compromising constitutional rights. The ambiguity in hazing laws,
combined with the continuance of hazing activities, has created
the call from many anti-hazing activists for the establishment of
national anti-hazing legislation. This legislation may create consistency in determining the legal threshold for hazing, as well as
the penalty for hazing. In 2005, a National Hazing Bill was proposed. This bill has failed to make it though the system. However,
the proposed bill has not been forgotten and many advocate groups
whose purpose is to help reduce hazing continue to try and lobby
for national hazing legislation.

Hazing as a Tradition

Hazing has been in existence since the time of ancient Greece.
As time has passed, these traditions have continued and evolved. In
modern times, if high school students are asked why they participated in hazing, they report that it "was fun and exciting." Other
reasons included "it brought us closer together as a team"; or "I got
to prove myself." Still other high school students report that "I had
to go through it last year, so now I get to do it to someone else," or
that it is a "tradition" (Hoover & Pollard, 2000). In fact, many
groups try to keep traditions alive by adding on to the traditions of
the past in order to leave their personal mark on the group. It is
this add-on effect that makes hazing more dangerous today than
in years past. By adding a new element to hazing, older experienced members get to add a new twist and expand on the tradition. For example, when a first-year athlete joined the team they were
required to drink a beer in order to become part of the team. The
following year, the new athletes were required to drink a six pack
of beer in order to become part of the team, as time passes the six-
pack becomes a gallon until the tradition becomes a "drink until you
pass out" rite of passage. The add-on effect has made hazing more

dangerous and some activities may be life threatening. Furthermore, hazing is typically planned and carried out behind closed doors or in secret. The silence is characteristically only broken after someone has been injured so severely that medical attention is required. At this point, the secret is revealed and the activities become public. The school or organization, as well as the athletes themselves, may be put under the media microscope and the effects of the hazing activity may be intensified by the amount of attention being given to the incident. This attention may cause great difficulty for the image of the school, its athletic programs, the coaches and the athletes, and thus becomes a public relations issue for the entire institution.

"Kids Will Be Kids: It's Middle School"

DP, an overweight sixth grade student in Michigan, had been the victim of physical and verbal bullying for several years. DP's parents reported the harassment only to be told by a school administrator, "Kids will be kids, its middle school." The parents responded by filing a Title IX suit naming the school district and superintendent as defendants for "failing to take reasonable action to halt or prevent such bullying." During the seventh grade, DP's locker was broken into and students "urinated on his clothing and threw his shoes into a toilet. His locker was also covered with sexually-oriented graffiti." DP's parents again reported the harassment and the students responsible were punished by school officials. This action helped for a time, however, other students continued to harass DP. Several months later, during a junior varsity baseball practice, DP was "sexually assaulted in the locker room by a teammate." DP reported the incident to his coach, who subsequently in a team meeting instructed team members, in the presence of DP, "not to joke around with a guy who can't take a man joke." Following this incident, DP transferred schools and took courses at a Catholic elementary school and at a local college. The U.S. District Court granted summary judgment to the defendants and the plaintiffs appealed. The appellate court held that school officials knew that the school's actions in the harassment were ineffective, but they continued to do the same thing over and over. The district court had ruled in favor of DP's parents, but kept summary judgment on the plaintiff's claim of "deliberate indifference" against the school district. As a result, the appellate court reversed the district court's ruling on "deliberate indifference." A federal jury then awarded $800,000 to DP's parents, the Pattersons, against the school district. *Patterson v. Hudson Area Schools and Mainar,* 551 F3d 438 (6th Cir. 2009).

High School Hazing

Hazing is often thought of as harmless fun, where "boys will be boys." This misconception can lead to troubling results. Hazing can be extremely harmful, especially during the middle school and high school years. Hazing at any age can be troublesome, but hazing in high school can have devastating hidden harms that often go unnoticed. Middle school and high school students are at various stages of development within their adolescence and are vulnerable to peer pressure due to their intense need to "belong" (Nuwer, 2000). We would all like to think that hazing is a thing of the past and that all the recent media attention regarding hazing has somewhat reduced the prevalence of hazing on our teams and at our schools. In an idealistic world, this would be the case; reality, however, sets in when you take a look at the recent headlines. For example, some recent headlines found in newspapers around the nation read as follows:

UTAH STUDENT HANDS IN GUILTY PLEA
FOR SEXUAL HAZING

• • •

COLORADO HIGH SCHOOL HIT WITH
SERIOUS HAZING ALLEGATIONS

• • •

FLORIDA SCHOOL SUSPENDS ATHLETES
PENDING INVESTIGATION;
COACH PUT ON LEAVE

• • •

HIGH SCHOOL STUDENT ALLEGEDLY HELD
DOWN AND ASSAULTED DURING HAZING

Hank Nuwer, one of the nation's foremost experts on hazing, states, "Hazing at any age can be exceedingly harmful. Hazing at the high school level is particularly troubling because the developmental stages of adolescence create a situation in which many students are more vulnerable to peer pressure due to the tremendous need for belonging, making friends and finding approval in one's peer group. Further, the danger of hazing at the high school level is heightened by the lack of awareness and policy development/enforcement around this issue. While many colleges and universities in the U.S. have instituted anti-hazing policies and educational awareness programs related to hazing, very few secondary schools have done the same" (Hanknuwer.com).

High School Hazing Statistics

Hazing is prevalent among American high school students.

- 48 percent of students who belong to groups reported being subjected to hazing activities.
- 43 percent reported being subjected to humiliating activities.
- 30 percent reported performing potentially illegal acts as part of their initiation. All high school students who join groups are at risk of being hazed.
- Both female and male students report high levels of hazing, although male students are at highest risk, especially for dangerous hazing.
- The lower a student's grade point average the greater their risk of being hazed.
- Almost every type of high school group had significantly high levels of hazing.
- Even groups usually considered safe haze new members. For example, 24 percent of students involved in church groups were subjected to hazing activities. Hazing hurts children, emotionally and physically.

- 71 percent of the students subjected to hazing reported negative consequences, such as getting into fights, being injured, fighting with parents, doing poorly in school, hurting other people, having difficulty eating, sleeping, or concentrating, or feeling angry, confused, embarrassed or guilty. Hazing starts young, and continues through high school and college.
- 25 percent of those who reported being hazed were first hazed before the age of 13.
- Dangerous hazing activities are as prevalent among high school students (22 percent) as among college athletes (21 percent).
- Substance abuse in hazing is prevalent in high school (23 percent) and increases in college (51 percent). Adults must share the responsibility when hazing occurs.
- Students were most likely to be hazed if they knew an adult who was hazed.
- 36 percent of the students said that they would not report hazing primarily because "There's no one to tell," or "Adults won't handle it right" (27 percent).
- Students do not distinguish between "fun" and hazing. Only 14 percent said they were hazed, yet 48 percent said they participated in activities that are defined as hazing, and 29 percent said they did things that are potentially illegal in order to join a group.
- Most said they participated in humiliating, dangerous or potentially illegal activities as a part of joining a group because those activities are "fun and exciting" (Pollard, 2005).

Hazing Leads to Girl's Suicide

Ashley Rogers, a 15-year-old sophomore at Glenn High School in Winston-Salem, NC, committed suicide by hanging herself at her home. Rogers, an academically talented student who excelled in extracurricular activities, had received "harassing text messages from other students." Rogers' death came three months after Phoebe Prince, a high school freshman in Massachusetts, committed suicide after months of harassment and death threats. Six of Prince's classmates have been charged with causing her death. In October

2006, Megan Meier, a student in Missouri, hung herself in a closet after she was "the target of cyber-bullying via her My Space account" (*News & Record*, April 17, 2010).

Hazing and Bullying Guidelines

The problems of hazing and bullying have continued to escalate and they are the cause of tremendous problems at all levels of athletics. In *Ethical Behavior in Sport*, we have included a chapter by Colleen McGlone on the problem of hazing. Specifically, she cites a case reviewed in the *Journal of Physical Education, Recreation and Dance* (2010) by Michael Carroll and Daniel P. Connaughton. In their article, Carroll and Connaughton discuss 10 risk management tips that are valuable for anyone who is responsible for creating a "zero-tolerance" bullying policy. These sport law experts detailed a serious bullying court case involving a sixth grade student that resulted in an $800,000 award by a federal jury (*Patterson v. Hudson Area Schools and Mainar*). Carroll and Connaughton recommend the following:

1. A strict, zero-tolerance anti-bullying and harassment policy should be developed and communicated to all stakeholders. Students and sport participants should know that bullying of any kind will not be tolerated and will result in strong disciplinary action.

2. The *Patterson* case illustrates that even some teachers at the school downplayed the bullying and harassment as normal joking behavior among students. Teachers, administrators and coaches need to be aware of the adverse effects of bullying, including depression, social isolation and suicidal thoughts.

3. Athletes and participants should be required to sign a contract.

4. Strong disciplinary and corrective measures should be taken for known cases of bullying. The consequences for such behavior should be used to dissuade other students from engaging in similar behaviors.

5. Ensure proper supervision of physical education classes, recess and after school or weekend sport activities. Research has shown that bullying often occurs in these settings due to a lack of proper supervision.

6. Establish an easy-to-implement reporting system, as well as a protocol for conducting fair investigations of reported bullying behavior.

7. Be aware of anti-bullying statutes that may exist in your state and make sure to comply with the legislation.

8. Keep a thorough record of reported instances of bullying and of the actions taken. Maintain these records for at least the length of time of the statute of limitations in your state.

9. Evaluate the school or organization's bullying practices and their effectiveness. The *Patterson* case demonstrates that an institution whose response to bullying has been proven to be ineffective yet keeps doing the same things may be found to be "deliberately indifferent" and could be held liable under Title IX.

10. Additional anti-bullying information may be obtained from the following websites:

> *www.stopbullyingnow.hrsa.gov/adults/*
> *www.schoolssafety.us*
> *www.naspoline.org*

Chapter 9

Act Now: Strategies for Improvement

JF:

OK, I'm finished criticizing administrators and complaining about the educational bureaucracy. It is time for me to practice what I preach, being goal-oriented and listing what I consider concrete recommendations dealing with improving public education in this country. There are all kinds of ideas about how to improve the educational system, with various political and social implications. My strategy is a simplistic approach that can be implemented immediately, with an alternative that is workable, albeit potentially controversial, and rooted in common sense based on the premise that the needs of the many outweigh the wants of the few. In order for the public school system in the United States to return to an efficient model for educating all children, our students must be held accountable for three things; attendance, behavior, and effort. Yes, I believe it really is that simple, because if those simple things are taken care of, everything else will fall into place. In my opinion, there is no need for fancy studies, blue ribbon commissions of educational experts, or consultants to correct our problems. We can do it ourselves — we must do it ourselves. There are, of course, those that will criticize my ideas but I'll wager that if you talk to the people on the front lines, the teachers in our classrooms — not the representatives of the NEA or the AFT, but the teachers — the overwhelming majority will agree that if these simple things are taken care of, the quality of education and climate in our schools will improve immediately, and that over time we will be able to eradicate many of the problems facing our schools, and that as our schools and students improve, our society will be the beneficiary. Read through my ideas, and then my ideas for students who choose not to participate, and decide for yourself whether or not this simple approach is worth trying. The bottom line is that something must be done—and done quickly to help our public schools.

Attendance Is a Key to Learning

First and foremost, students need to be in school, and they need to be in class. This is a "no-brainer." Learning cannot take place in an empty desk. If a child is not sick, they need to be in school, and if they are sick, they need to be at home. Unfortunately, there are some schools with ridiculous attendance policies that basically force parents to send ill children to school, thereby spreading sickness among a wider range of students. If a child has a 102 temperature, they need to be in bed, not in a classroom. Teachers are more than willing to make sure that absent students have the proper assignments to make up missed work, and students can do a good job of helping each other get caught up by simply working together. The schools need to do a good job of communicating with parents, and parents need to do a good job of holding their children accountable for being in school and ensuring that they do what they are supposed to do following absences. In addition, schools need to have common sense attendance policies that take into account that students are going to be ill and may have to miss school. Truancy is another problem. Most states and school districts have policies on truancy, and many are supposed to hold parents accountable in some fashion for the actions of their children. My question is, are these policies enforced? At the school level, hold kids accountable for their actions with creative punishment. Talk with teachers to devise ways to encourage kids to be in class and the consequences for not being in class. And districts must have common-sense policies dealing with the unexcused absences of students. If students skip a certain number of times, they will not get credit—that's it. And the student who is not going to get credit does not get to sit in the back of that classroom and be disruptive. Areas can be determined where these students can be placed to work on individual assignments—if they choose to. I'll wager that after the first round of these disciplinary measures, many of the students who have to do this will not want to do it again. In my years of teaching, I have had to deal with numerous attendance policies that have little or no accountability distinction between an excused lawful absence and whether a student skipped the class. This is ludicrous! Hold them accountable.

HA:

Attendance Is Essential

From the time I taught the 8th grade until the time I taught graduate students who were working toward their terminal degrees, I was passionate that students attend classes.

At every level of my teaching, I stressed the importance of being in class. One of the things I still feel good about was that our students bought in to my request that they attend every class. At Guilford College I had excellent attendance and even at the classes for the Masters Degree and Doctorate attendance was phenomenal. Students at the graduate level would call from the highway to tell me that they had car trouble so I could know they were not cutting class. It can be done! Like Joe Franks, I believe so strongly that students can't learn unless they are in class. At Guilford, three of my students told me that they went to a class known to be difficult to get the syllabus of the course. The only time they attended class was to take a periodic test. Their professor told them he never required attendance and their grade would depend solely on test scores. All three received A's as their grade without attending class. I assured them that they had chosen the low road and in all probability had missed many valuable lessons. I also remember a student major recalling that his professor had told his class that he never required them to come to class and would not use attendance as a factor in their grade. The student missed several classes, but thought it would not affect his grade. His test scores were a strong B but to his surprise and disappointment, he received a C. When he questioned his professor about the C, he was told he took points off because he missed too many classes. Not fair, but the C stood.

JF:

Appropriate Behavior Is Crucial to the Success of the School

If we are successful in having students in attendance, what is the next critical factor we must deal with? The behavior of students in class and in school is crucial. From day one in the public schools, children should be taught what is acceptable and unacceptable behavior with regard to their interpersonal relationships and their interaction with authority figures. Unfortunately, society has given students very poor examples of how to interact. In addition, many students get very poor examples from their families. When I first started teaching and a student did something in class that I felt needed to be corrected, I was able to say, "You don't do that at home do you?" Their typical answer was no and we were able to move on with the fact they could not do that in school either. What I have seen develop over the years is that many behaviors that are allowed to go on in the home are inappropriate and unacceptable at school. These behaviors should not and must not be allowed to go on at school—plain and simple. I'm sorry that some of these children have to deal with poor environments, but the bottom line is that there are certain things that will NOT be tolerated in certain environments, and the sooner that our children learn that, the better we will all be. One only need to use the example of yelling fire in a crowded area or making jokes about having weapons in airports. Not many people engage in these behaviors for two reasons. The mores of our society have made it quite clear that this is not to be done, and there are swift consequences for this type of behavior. Of course, we always need to be tolerant of cultural differences with regard to certain types of interactions and behaviors.

Nevertheless, students and parents need to understand what is appropriate and acceptable in a school environment. Many young people today think that the way we communicate with one another is at the top of the voice in challenging tones and that fighting with others is a perfectly acceptable way of resolving conflict. I remember seeing a bizarre event in the office at our school after two girls had a fight on the way to school on the bus. When they were brought to the office and their parents were called to pick them up, the parents got into a shouting match in the office and had to be restrained before blows were thrown. The saying about the "apple not falling far from the tree" really does apply in most cases. Kids will reflect what they learn, and if parents aren't going to do it, then we must. Unfortunately for a growing number of our students, we have people that aren't parents—they simply produced children. Yet young people get as many behavioral messages from the media as any other source. Media plays a huge role in the lives of kids, and more often than not, kids are getting questionable examples from mass media. In my opinion, young people are taking behavioral cues from a media that celebrates dysfunction and incivility. One can use the old excuse that the media is merely reflecting what goes on in society—well, then we as educators must take a stand to communicate what is appropriate.

The Most Important Lesson

With regard to student behavior, I have the firm belief that the most important thing we can teach young people in school is to initially comply with the direction of authority. Think about this for a minute—if people in this society would initially comply with the direction of authority, so many problems and famous incidents that have caused social upheaval could be avoided. I'm not talking about blindly following all directions, but there is a time and a place for questioning and argument. In school, if a teacher asks a student to do something, and that request is not illegal or immoral, then the student should comply. If they have a problem with that, go talk to an administrator and express their concern. This should be taught from day one. Unfortunately, our society teaches people to have contempt for authority and to question authority. What if—just what if—Rodney King had initially complied with the directions of the police officers in L.A.? Would that savage beating have taken place? I venture to guess no. We are totally missing a window of opportunity to make society a more tolerant and civil place to live and use the public schools as the agent of socialization to teach positive behaviors. And for those of you ready to accuse me of conservative social engineering through the schools with regard to behavior, get a grip—free-wheeling, no-consequence social policies have helped contribute to the problems we face now.

HA:

UBI Sunt!

When I was at Wakelon High School in Zebulon, North Carolina, football began on a limited schedule because many of our athletes were priming tobacco and were progressing as well as could be expected working with tobacco. One of the most talented players was in Canada and missed the pre-season workouts. He was due to arrive a week after the opening of school and I looked forward to his joining our small squad. I was walking down the hallway at school when a young man stopped me and said "Medlin's the name, what is yours?" There was a smugness, almost arrogance in his voice and it irritated me since we both knew who each other was although we had never met. I simply said, "Herb Appenzeller," and kept on walking. Later that day, Jim Medlin came into Latin class and swaggered to a front row seat looking bored. During the lesson, Medlin let out the loudest yawn I believe I ever heard and looked around for the approval of the class. No one seemed supportive of his conduct and I quietly asked him to step outside in the hall. When he came out I grabbed him by the shirt and slammed him hard against the wall. In a calm voice that betrayed my anger, I warned him such conduct would not be tolerated, not then or ever. He was shocked and frightened and assured me it would never happen again. Prior to the start of practice that day, I told my for-

mer teammate from Wake Forest about the incident that morning and how I planned to retaliate at practice and teach Jim Medlin
a lesson he would never forget. We put him through rough drills
to see how much he could take. Dick Kelly, who volunteered his
services as line coach until he entered medical school in January,
taught me a valuable lesson. "What he does off the field or in the
classroom has nothing to do with his performance at football practice," he angrily told me. Treat him without prejudice and on his
effort on the practice field. I needed that advice and I accepted
and followed it as long as I taught and coached. In fact, Jim Medlin
is the only student that I grabbed and pushed against a wall. I re-
gretted that! Jim Medlin expected some type of retaliation and
punishment and was surprised and relieved when none came. He
gave us a great effort and had a tremendous attitude that earned
him the respect of his teammates and coaches. We had a great season although we were very few in number. By midseason we were
ranked 13th in the state of North Carolina's football poll. In those
days all schools no matter what size or classification were ranked
by the *Raleigh News and Observer*. We had a strong offense that
scored easily until our small squad was depleted with injuries as we
faced the county's largest school in the season finale. Our quarterback was out and a second-string quarterback would be forced
to take over although his claim to fame was his ability to play the
guitar and sing country and western music. Our squad was so
hampered with injuries, I called in the seniors and told them we
would cancel the game. They had worked too hard and too well to
be crushed by a strong team due to our injuries. The seniors could
not believe my suggestion and quickly responded that quitting
would be against everything I taught them and ruin their season.
"If we get defeated we can live with it, but we can't live with quitting." I agreed to their wishes. The game was important and one
in which I had a lot to prove. I had turned down a lucrative offer
of salary, perks, a large veteran squad, a great stadium and other
incentives to go to a school that had a tradition of losing in all
sports. Now my 14 men would be put to the test against 55 men
who would be out to prove I was wrong in rejecting that offer to
coach them. I told the members of the team to space themselves

ten yards apart when they ran on the field so it would appear that we had more numbers. We did, and then the green and white jerseys of 55 raced on the field. I got our men in the pregame huddle on sidelines, desperately trying to find the right words for an extremely difficult situation. Suddenly Jim Medlin stepped in front of the huddle and shouted, "Look at them, Coach, we are just like the ancient Romans, we don't care how big they are or how many there are, we just want to say, Ubi Sunt! Where are they." He remembered the stories and mythology of the Latin class when I talked about the fighting spirit of the Romans who said to an enemy soldier who taunted them, "We will shoot so many arrows into the sky and throw so many javelins that you won't see the sun!" The Roman responded "then we'll fight in the shade." Medlin was paying attention in class and learned his lessons well, capturing the fighting spirit of the ancient Romans. I could not improve on a pep talk and let "Ubi Sunt" be our battle cry. It was the last game for our seniors who wanted to go out winners. They played inspired football and tied the score at 6–6 late in the game. In desperation, our opponent threw a late pass and scored. There was pass interference and the official did not pull his flag and my heart sank. I thought it just isn't fair to a group of men who have played their hearts out. Suddenly the hometown official threw the flag nullifying the touchdown. I gained tremendous respect for officials that day when the home crowd wanted the touchdown and verbally attacked his call. We did not win, but neither did we lose. The game ended in a tie and in this instance, I accepted the tie as a victory. Our fans were ecstatic since they realized the tremendous odds that faced us while the home fans of our opponent were bitter over the loss because they had been heavily favored. Several weeks after that game a good coach was fired. There is little doubt that a Jim Medlin, "Ubi Sunt" band of determined men gave an inspired performance that unfortunately led to the firing of a coach. I felt lucky that I turned that job down and elected to take a job a smaller school without the advertised advantages. I also realized that Dick Kelly gave me good advice regarding discipline and stereotyping individuals. It was a lesson well learned.

JF:

Character Is Crucial

As I mentioned earlier, under a previous central administration, there was a district and community initiative to add a cross-curricular character education component in the schools. Based on a national model, this started with a local committee that identified what they considered cornerstones of character to be promoted throughout the school system. These represented important traits that should be taught and nurtured. They included integrity, self-discipline, determination, giving, and caring. Excellent character traits that, if developed, could be great contributors to an individual's success in life. These were identifiable concepts and behaviors that children could be taught and that could be nurtured throughout the educational process. Individual schools held conferences where they brought in students from across the district to come together to talk about issues affecting the schools and how the development of these traits could make a difference for people. The early focus was to start with elementary students and continue to build throughout their educational career. I felt that this was a great idea, and a needed one. But I was in the minority. Because of poor communication from the district, many teachers saw this as merely another bureaucratic buzzword program and did not buy into what could have been very positive. The program basically died when a new superintendent came in with his own agenda that did not include teaching the students in our system positive character traits. Unbelievable. And another superb example of an educational bureaucrat ignoring what in the long run could have been one of the most important programs in our system. A catch phrase of the Character Education program was "You Know What's Right — DO IT!" I loved this slogan and still have it up in my classroom. In fact, on numerous occasions, I have given a sticker with the slogan on it to a kid and told them to put it on the mirror in their room as a reminder to make good decisions — much like wearing a W.W.J.D. bracelet, I suppose. I believed in my heart that kids really did know what was right, appropriate and acceptable. I still believe that, but over the years I have observed that kids make some really stupid decisions, and yes, so do the adults. In fact, there is a poster in the front of my classroom, made for me by students, that shows a favorite slogan and one of my best pieces of advice for students — "Don't be an Idiot." Unfortunately, the "gray area" with regard to behavior grows with each passing year, and there is a growing divide between what is right morally and what is acceptable and tolerated in our society. In one of my classes, we talk about the sociologist Robert Merton, who attempted to explain a cause of deviant behavior using a concept he termed anomie, a situation where the norms of society become unclear. Over the past few years, when we get into discussions in class about various issues and the students begin to give their ideas about what is OK and not OK, invariably I will blurt out, Robert Merton was right! (Much in the same way as saying "Howard Johnson is right," and if you don't know what I'm talking about, you are culturally deprived — go rent *Blazing Saddles*.) Of course, I have to explain why I think Merton was right in this situation, but some of the decisions that young people make today are due to the huge gray area we have in this society regarding what is acceptable and unacceptable. If I'm walking down the hall behind a group of students, and they don't know that I'm there, they will act and talk naturally. Perhaps one of them is reciting the lyrics to one of the popular "songs" of the day and lets a few expletives fly. When I try to correct them, sometimes their rationalization for why it's OK to say that is because "it's in a song" or "man, I was just rappin." Regardless, I try to explain to them that it is unacceptable to say that and they should not. Usually, they are embarrassed and will say OK — but the ones that are belligerent have the opportunity to be escorted to the office for a more thorough explanation from a member of the administration. A critical problem we deal with lies in an environment where kids don't necessarily think they are doing anything wrong, because they probably have never been told that it is wrong, and even if they have, it has never been reinforced. We tolerate way too much unacceptable behavior in this society and in our schools as free expression, or the fact that these are kids. This needs to change!

Thankfully, as I ended my career, a new superintendent has brought the Character Education component back to the system—I hope it stays.

HA:

New Trends for 21st Century Education
- Use of Technology and iPad's challenges and solutions
- Online Education
- "Race to the Top" Grants: 900 districts apply for grants
- "No Child Left Behind"
- Community College: Remediation is Costly
- New Trends in Video Use
- School Lunches Get a 21st Century Makeover
- Cyberbullying and Legislation
- Techbooks ($45 per yr.) v. Textbooks ($100 per yr.); Techbooks include training for teachers
- Use of SKYPE.COM
- Evaluation of teachers, principals, and superintendents
- Charter schools draw students from private schools (*eSchool News*, Oct. 2012)

Two current examples are:

1) **iPads**

iPads engage students to take ownership in their learning. The goal for teachers is meeting the needs of each and every child. Gifted students need to be challenged to reach their potential. What is the best way to achieve this goal? In same school districts they vary from "inclusion or pull out." In some elementary schools inclusion refers to clustering the gifted in a class where they are taught together: AIG, Academically and Intellectually Gifted.

2)   Race to the Top Grants

The U.S. Department of Education has approximately 900 school districts applying for a "Race to the Top" grant. The federal government has set aside $400 million for grants to school districts "in support of local initiators that help close achievement gaps and prepare students for college and career" (*eSchool News*, Oct. 2012). Arne Duncan, Education Secretary, commented on the grants when he said, "I believe the best ideas come from leaders at the local level." President Obama "has awarded $400 billion to 18 states and the District of Columbia." The grants have had a positive effect on education reform, "encouraging charter schools and changing how teachers are evaluated" (*eSchool News*, Oct. 2012). The competitive grants "encourage districts to create learning environments that are aligned with college and career ready standards, accelerate student achievement, and expand access to the most effective teachers" (*eSchool News*, Oct. 2012). The "Race to the Top" grants require 40 percent of the students to come from low income families to qualify. "In addition, the districts must provide by 2013–2014 evaluations for teachers, principals, and superintendents. Another requirement to qualify for a grant is "to provide instructors with data on student growth." Alberto Carvalho, Superintendent of Miami-Dade Public Schools in Florida said:

> The states awarded Race to the Top funds would give at the district level, the ability to achieve rapid and catalytic transformation to the local level without a state process to be navigated (*eSchool News*, Oct. 2012).

Carvalho also noted that:

> The districts application will focus on personalized education for students based on

how best they learn, rely more on digital content, and changing the learning environment and outcomes of middle school students who have fallen behind.

Carvalho concluded, "This is a creative and effective way of spurring reform from the bottom up" (*eSchool News*, Oct. 2012).

JF:

A word of caution here with regard to "free" money from the federal government. While a concept may have potential positives, the unintended consequences that Herb and I have found over the years rears its head again here. In my last year, our school system, after receiving additional funding, was scrambling to meet "surprise" requirements to have standardized tests in all subjects. What would this mean? An additional layer of bureaucracy to create these tests for all subjects, including electives. Funding is great, but the strings attached can be very long and tangled.

Chapter 10

Is It Really That Bad?

JF:

Young people today are worldlier than any generation before them. We can thank technology, a couple of generations of more liberal parenting, more liberal standards in the media and a more liberal society in general. Things that were taboo a few generations ago are now commonplace—and what's next? I believe this occurs because someone or some group "pushes the envelope" to see what they can get away with and the behavior is not challenged or corrected consistently by society. It is human nature to push the envelope—to strive for more—or to push and see what one can get away with. When we discuss this concept in class, I try to use examples that the kids can relate to. In the mid-1980s, the Fox television network came out with a groundbreaking and very successful animated series—*The Simpsons*. I remember the huge uproar that followed *The Simpsons* from parent and teacher groups because the underachieving Bart Simpson was such a terrible role model for kids. When that furor died down, as so many things do, it was time for someone to push the envelope. MTV obliged by bringing us *Beavis and Butthead*. These two morons made Bart Simpson look like an angel. I must admit that I laughed out loud at their ridiculous exploits (I still haven't grown up). Yet, this program was never intended for young children. Invariably, kids were going to copy some of the stupid things depicted on the show, and parent groups were up in arms and wanted to pull it off the air. When the furor died down, someone was there to pick up the slack and push the envelope again. Comedy Central's *South Park* (yes, I laugh at this one too), has not only pushed an envelope, it has let the proverbial genie out of the bottle. The language and situations depicted on this show makes one wonder what those in the FCC do for a living. Situations and language that would get an R or NC-17 movie rating are on a general cable network all the time. And this trend of walking the fine line of acceptability has spread onto more general television with animated programs like *Family Guy*. My point is that the more our standards are pushed, and the more that genie gets out of the bottle with regard to what is acceptable and tolerated, the more the decision making is skewed with young people. Add to that a steady dose of Jerry Springer, Dave Chappelle and YouTube and you have a great stew to influence the behavior of students. You see, Robert Merton was right and we have a state where the norms of society are not clearly defined and this has helped to push our culture to more forms of what my grandmother would call "crude, rude and unacceptable." I'm really not a prude with the type of entertainment that I enjoy, but I will stand firm that there is a time and a place for everything and very often things are brought into school that are inappropriate. It's not the time or the place. In addition, the seniors that I teach are more mature than elementary or middle schoolers. My methods and topics that have worked for me for 30 years would not work nearly as well with younger students.

Chapter 11

Going to School Is a Right—Being at My School Is a Privilege

JF:

With regard to behavior in schools, students are not going to be little angels all the time. To be blunter, you are going to find jerks from every socioeconomic, racial and ethnic background. There will always be some students who are going to be disrespectful and disruptive. Well folks, unruly students have no right to disrupt the educational environment for the overwhelming majority of students who come to school and, for the most part, do what they are supposed to do. Students who consistently choose to disrupt school do not need to be in a regular educational setting—they need to be placed in an alternative school. We are depriving the majority of our students and our teachers for that matter, a positive educational and work environment where real learning can take place. Students that choose to disrupt the educational environment in our schools have no right to infringe upon the rights of those who are there to learn in relative conformity. The needs of the many do outweigh the needs of the few in this case and until this critical issue is addressed, our public schools will not improve and we will see the continued exodus of students from our public schools.

I fully realize that this is probably the most controversial component of my plan to help our educational system — the creation of alternative middle and high schools for students who simply will not conform. I do believe that it's our own fault for every kid we lose to private, parochial and charter schools because we are not meeting the needs of the many in a positive learning environment. And what do you think causes this type of flight from our public schools? The reputation for undisciplined and disruptive educational environments that detract from the function of education. Many parents have little faith that the schools will get any better and the ones that can afford to move will continue to do so. Some communities have created voucher programs so that students can basically escape a failing school. But why in the world are we not addressing the problem at the source? We must make our schools better — and NOW. Young people that can't conform in a regular school can attend another one that will meet their special behavioral needs. And don't give me any of this claptrap about how children have a right to attend any school. They are very able to attend a school and receive as much education as they will accept — they just won't be here. Just as free speech is only free until the rights of others are violated, attending my school is a privilege that can be lost. I'm not advocating a "Joe Clark" approach with a baseball bat and bullhorn, although that was inspiring (if you don't recognize this reference, again you are culturally deprived — go rent *Lean on Me*). What I am suggesting is based on the fact that alternative or optional schools already exist in some school districts, and I feel that their scope needs to be expanded. What is taught and how it is taught there can be debated, but the needs of the many require us to make this type of commitment to securing the educational environment in our schools.

This type of drastic action will also have the intended consequence of sending an important message to what I call the "fence sitters" in our schools. These are young people who basically could go either way — they can conform to accepted standards, or they can choose to be disruptive. These young people have not matured emotionally or socially to the point where they can independently do what they should. Like Judge Smails, we need to ask, "What do you stand for Danny, goodness or badness?" (And if you don't know who Judge Smails was, you are culturally deprived — go rent *Caddyshack*.) If a "fence sitter" sees kids get away with something, they will be inclined to try it too. If nothing is done to the students who are disrupting our schools, it sends a message that there are no consequences to this behavior and the situation gets worse. Yet, if these students see that there are consequences to unacceptable behavior, and that those consequences are not enjoyable, most will tend to move toward conformity. This demonstrates the sociological concept of differential association, which in layman's terms states that if you hang around a bunch of jerks, chances are that you will probably end up acting like a jerk. I tell my students that parents believe in the validity of this concept and they understand exactly what I am talking about. As we all grew up, there were certain kids that our parents didn't want us hanging around or going out with, because they didn't want us to act like them. Folks, the "fence sitters" exist in great numbers, they are the ones we need to reach and the sooner we do, the sooner our schools will start to improve. It is with these students where we will see immediate short-term improvement — it is over time as we create consistency of expectations that will see the resurgence of our educational system.

The third component of my model to improve our educational system deals with effort — plain and simple. I once worked with a coach who told his players that they didn't have to be a talented athlete to give good effort, and he was right. ANY kid can give good effort — they have to try; to participate in class; to do their homework; and to take responsibility for work that they miss when they are out of school. We need to teach students at an early age to be conscientious, responsible and have self-discipline. This is where that cross-curricular character education can make a difference. Reward good effort — don't just reward good grades. Not every child is an "A" student, regardless of what their parent thinks. If a "C" is the best that student can do in a particular class, then reward and praise them for doing their best. It is the job of parents and teachers to push young people to do their best, but to temper that push with a healthy dose of realistic expectations. And for that matter, not every high school graduate is destined to go to a four-year college as well. We need to understand that there is a place for occupational education, and admit that vocational education has been passed over in many a school district in this country. There is, and has been, a demand for quality skilled labor in this society, and for someone who is competent in a trade, they can make a good living and support their family. Unfortunately, our society tends to look down on vocational education in schools and that is a disservice to many students who could use this as a way to be successful in life.

While my ideas will be criticized by some educational "experts" and politicians, I again challenge someone to tell me how my common sense approach to making attendance, behavior and effort priorities to improving public education will not dramatically and effectively restore our school system to greatness. If a student is in school, acts right and does their best, academic achievement will take care of itself. But this needs be drilled in from day one. I firmly believe that these common sense suggestions will make a difference in the lives of students, the parents of those students, and improve the working environment for teachers by creating an environment of civility and achievement in education.

Chapter 12

Let's Address and Correct Perceived Problems

JF:

I don't know about your school and community situation, but in mine, the political hot potato relates to a gap in the levels of achievement between minority and white students. Does one exist? Yes, in some cases it does. Depending on what part of the country you are in, one would find disparities in achievement between students whether Asian, African American, White, Latino, Native American—you name it. This is a multifaceted problem with no easy solution. I'm thrilled to see in my community a step toward an emphasis in early childhood education focusing on preparation to entering the public schools. This problem will take generations to address, but let's be candid—children have different skills and abilities and will never be one homogeneous group across the board when it comes to performance. I believe that this gap can be dealt with effectively if students follow my three suggestions of being in school, acting in acceptable ways and trying their best from day one in the school. When we invest in young people at every level and hold students and their parents accountable for these three things, the gap should decrease dramatically. And it doesn't matter what race or ethnic group a student belongs to—if they don't come to school, behave and give good effort—they will not be successful. Sound like a broken record? Good. Quit blaming me as a teacher and the system for everyone's problems and start making personal responsibility a priority. The bottom line reality that I have observed is that many young people who are the "victims" of this gap are typically those that do not attend regularly, are disruptive in class and are not prepared each and every day to be successful. Where the system has failed is when students have been socially promoted into grades and classes that they are not ready for—an "educational Peter Principle," so to speak. This practice must stop, because we are hurting the young people that we are supposedly trying to help. This is a major unintended consequence of educational policy in the United States that, in my opinion, is addressable and correctable.

Discipline in the School Setting

Over my years in public education, one thing that is particularly disturbing to me is the notion that teachers are not being sensitive to children who misbehave. Perhaps, if we take enough workshops we'll understand and dismiss or ignore the disrespectful, belligerent and disruptive student behavior. The bottom line is that students who exhibit these behaviors need to be disciplined. It makes my blood boil when I have taken a student to an administrator only to hear, "Well, they are really improved over where they were last year!" This isn't last year, and please quit rationalizing and making excuses for a student's poor behavior.

There obviously is no "one size fits all" approach to discipline. A generation ago, out-of-school suspension was something to be avoided at all costs. There was a stigma associated with it. For many students today, it is perceived as a vacation from school—the stigma is gone. If a student must be suspended outside of school, make suspensions mean something. For example, if you have a certain number of suspension days, you can finish the term in an alternative school setting and reapply for admission to the traditional school for the next session. Any decent alternative school would have the base curriculum, along with classes on character and behavioral norms, and a rigid disciplinary structure to encourage students to engage in behaviors that will keep them in the traditional school. In addition, if the teaching of technical and vocational competencies would be desirable and beneficial to the student, this might be an appropriate half-way step to a more traditional setting.

With regard to suspension of students, there is the invariable complaining that certain students are singled out for suspension. Right behind the achievement gap argument is the disproportionate suspension argument with regard to minority students. Let me give you a radical idea for cutting the number of suspensions—OBEY THE RULES! I remember earlier in my career when a directive came from on high in the superintendent's office that schools needed to cut the number of suspensions. Well, we cut the number of suspensions alright, but did the students really act any better—absolutely not. Thank goodness this directive was short-lived. What kind of message does that send to students, parents and especially staff? Remember when I spoke of the "fence sitters" and their propensity to follow negative behavior that had little or no accountability? Enough said. But there is a deeper problem, the fact that when students are not disciplined, teacher morale drops, and then teachers ignore undesirable behavior because they lack the faith that something will be done. This is a vicious circle that pulls schools down and it must be addressed. If kids misbehave, discipline them—secure the integrity of the teaching environment.

I have always tried to be the kind of teacher who will try to talk to a student and ask them to comply as opposed to "playing the heavy." I have found that this works well individually and in groups where kids are more likely to "show out" in front of their friends when they feel they are being challenged. When it doesn't work well, when a student chooses to ignore me or is disrespectful, that was when I would escort him or her to a member of the administration. And please don't try to tell me WHY they act the way they do in an attempt to rationalize their boorish behavior as I have had some administrators try to do. I'll be very honest to the student in front of the administrator, "You know, nobody will ever hassle you on this campus when you do what you are supposed to do. It's when you do something that you are not supposed to that you call attention to yourself and start this process." I have yet to understand why this is such a complicated concept for some students. We can be concerned about our students' self-esteem and be very nurturing, but let us never abdicate out disciplinary responsibilities. This authoritative approach, I have found, is a successful strategy.

HA:

On discipline I agree with Joe Franks. I remember supervising my student teachers at a junior high school that had a tremendous success rate and a school that had order that created an environment conducive to learning. Our student teachers benefitted from such an environment that gave them the opportunity to teach. A few years later the complete opposite was the norm and chaos was the rule. The teachers spent their teaching time attempting, and in most instances not succeeding, to maintain order so they could teach. What was once a proud and effective school became a teacher's nightmare. At any level the learning process must be accompanied by discipline that allows teaching to go on. In my third year of teaching I had a very caring and effective principal who had the welfare of his students and teaching the number one priority. Everyone knew the guidelines and also the fact that his strength was creating an environment that fostered good teaching. One day he shared a concern that troubled him — an average student who had stayed in elementary school for too long. He was the oldest student in his class and someone who caused trouble everyday. My principal told me that "Ben" (fictional name) had been voted president of his class, a fact that our principal could not understand. Ben, of all the students, could not possibly be president. The principal interviewed several of Ben's classmates and learned that every morning before school started, at recess, and after school, Ben would take two students at a time to the room where the furnace was located and dig under a pile of coats where he had a gun. He told his classmates that he would kill them if they did not vote for him for president. The vote was unanimous. Ben was subjected to many sessions where the principal's belt was used. I was asked to witness such a punishment when the belt was used. Ben never made a comment although the whipping was so severe that I told the principal not to ask me again to be his witness to such punishment. If taken to court by Ben's parents for his excessive punishment, I told him I could not testify on the principal's behalf because of the severity of the punishment.

Finally, in frustration, my principal asked if I would let him join the football team with the hope that the sport could change his attitude and daily problems. Of course, I agreed and he became a member of our football team. I did not know what to expect, but soon felt that he was a changed person. Ben's attitude was excellent, he was with boys his age and he had a new interest to help him enjoy school.

The experiment worked and his brother, also a number of the team, was excited over Ben's transformation. After my two years at the school, I accepted a position at Chowan College in Murfreesboro, North Carolina and lost touch with Ben.

The Longest Steal of Home in Baseball History

One morning I read in a local newspaper that a new record had been established for "the longest steal of home in baseball history." The record was set by a person named Ben who was playing baseball for a juvenile detention team. He jumped over the outfield fence as he rounded the bases and commandeered a car and made the driver take him home 35 miles from the detention home for a new record.

Ben had made progress and never terrorized his classmates, but unfortunately the good deeds did not last long enough. Corporal punishment did not work for some and I remember that discipline in the schools I attended in Newark, New Jersey had minimal disciplinary problems even though the state of New Jersey prohibited corporal punishment for all students. It is imperative that schools at all levels find the best method to maintain discipline — without discipline it is difficult to provide an environment that provides the best teaching.

JF:

What to Do with the 9th Grade

In our system, we have a 9th–12th high school curriculum and thus the middle school 6th–8th curriculum, as opposed to the junior high 7th–9th model. Years ago, I really thought that when the middle school format was adopted and the 9th grade came to the high school, that it would be good for them. I felt that the 9th graders were too "big" for junior high and that the seniors would ensure that they would stay under control. As I have stated earlier, what I have found is that the freshmen come to our campus feeling great about themselves, but many cannot follow directions and have not been held accountable at the middle school level. It is almost like they have never had to follow directions and could do whatever they wanted. Consequently, in my school, the overwhelming majority of our discipline problems occur in the 9th grade, and there are too many 9th grade repeaters each year. Some of them simply do not have the self discipline necessary to be successful in our academic environment. This is unfortunate, because I still believe that they belong at the high school level. I also believe, however, that if my ideas about effort and behavioral expectations were adopted in the middle school, we would reduce the number of problems and these 9th grade students and they would find a new measure of success as they begin high school.

Competencies as Standards

When minimum basic competencies are established in each and every grade, and students are held accountable for meeting those minimum standards before they are promoted to the next grade, this will be the most meaningful educational reform in a century. And as I have said previously, there are those that will say that we are going to stigmatize and emotionally scar the child that is retained in a lower grade, but in the long run, I contend this is better for the child in that we will have children in schools that can be put in a position to be successful — in each and every grade. This is education as it should be. The most difficult strategic part of this plan is that it is longitudinal—a long-term approach. In reality, the most difficult part of the plan will be the political firestorm it will create in the short term. A critical question becomes what to do with students already in the system. While this will be the subject of intense debate, I personally feel that students in the K–5 area can handle immediate implementation of these reforms with the least amount of social stigma adjustment. Strategies would need to be implemented for students in middle and high schools with regard to intense remediation for those who lack basic competencies. In addition, with many states going to some type of exit examination required for graduation, let these students and parents know of the intentions for these to be concrete with at least 3 years of advance notice. That would satisfy transition in middle school and high school. I am reminded of the parents in South Florida a few years ago who balked and cried discrimination with regard to exit exams that were trying to be immediately implemented. This would have immediately resulted in many students not meeting the requirements to graduate from high school. There are two ways to look at this situation—from the critical perspective, one could say that if the students couldn't pass, they shouldn't graduate. From the nurturing perspective, if these students were socially promoted without achieving basic competencies needed for a reasonable chance for success beyond high school, then there should have been remediation programs established to ensure that these kids could perform these tasks. If the programs were not available, they should be given the benefit of the doubt. Neither is an adequate solution to a problem that was years in the making.

You might remember my story about when I first started teaching, I had two classes of what was called United States History Workshop. This was a skills level class for students who had below a fifth grade reading level. That's right—11th and 12th graders who had below a fifth grade reading level. It was my feeling then, and it is now, that this class was important for these students because you had to put kids in an environment where they could learn something and experience a level of success. Because many of these students were minority students, I taught a basic overview of U.S. History, with an emphasis on Black History as a motivator. I tried to integrate life skills such as basic world geography, map skills with an emphasis on the highway system, along with newspaper and current event activities. Yes, this was in the days before the internet was in our school. The students I had in this class had lost confidence in their ability to achieve in school and were skeptical with regard to me and this class. Instead of telling these students what they heard most often from too many teachers at the beginning of a school year — "If you don't do this, this and this, you will flunk" — I told them very simply, "If you do this, this and this, you will pass" — and I meant it. I knew that if they would come to class, give me a decent effort and do what they were supposed to do, they would experience success. And they did. And I'll tell you another thing — this class was full of "fence sitters" with a sprinkling of the "troublemakers." Some of the historical "troublemakers" didn't last very long, but the ones that hung in there did a decent job and I had very little problems from these students. These classes were intentionally small, 15–17 students, but for many of the students that could have been problems, they definitely were not and I had a most satisfying experience teaching them.

As I look back on that experience, and for that matter my career, one thing I remember as being so unfortunate is that when we would have parent visitation nights, almost no parents showed up for these class periods — and these were the students who needed that support the most! I'll bet if you asked most teachers about these parent nights, in most of their classes, the parents that showed up most often were those whose kids were the conforming performers. The students who needed that parental involvement the most were most often neglected. Teachers know there is a direct correlation between parental involvement and student behavior and performance. We need to encourage parental involvement — from both the school and community levels. Although it can't be required, we should work with community groups, utilize public service announcements in the media and every means available to challenge and encourage parents to be parents and get involved in the lives of their kids. One of my recent principals did a really good job of reaching out to communities and doing her best to work with parents.

Reflecting back on the Florida test situation, I can understand how parents would have been upset if some type of exit test was "sprung" on them, but how can a parent in good conscience lay the blame totally on the state because their child can't perform? Herein lies another key component of the problem facing public education—not accepting personal responsibility for one's actions. If people know expectations well enough in advance, and clear indicators are given for achievement as one progresses through school, fuss all you want, but if you can't pass, you can't advance or graduate. Again, if we take care of business from day one, the big picture will fall into place!

HA:

Play: It's How Kids Learn Social Skills

The Federal Centers for Disease Control and Prevention started a "Move It Outdoors" campaign to combat the lack of outdoor play. The Centers found that "a child is six times more likely to play a video game than ride a bike on a typical day." The Center also reports that "children spend less time than ever playing outdoors, exploring and just being kids." Dr. Nannette Funderburk, a therapist in Greensboro, North Carolina, said: "Sometimes it's just easier to put on a movie or put on a video game." Glenn Hodgson, an elementary school teacher and father of two children commented on play:

> Children who are permitted to play freely with peers develop the skill of seeing things through another person's point of view—cooperating, helping, sharing and solving problems.

Dr. Funderburk recommends play when she writes:

> Play can later affect how a person's interests in work, social situations or adult relationships. It actually im-

pacts social and emotional development because *the playground is where we practice for life.*

Brian Williams on NBC News, August 7, 2012 reported "80% of women executives played team sports according to a recent survey." Funderburk continues with her support of play, saying:

> A growing number of child care centers are moving in the direction of the research which promotes more simplified play that promotes creativity.

It is apparent that play like that we support in co-curricular activities meets the goals of educators like Joe Franks (*News & Record*, August 4, 2012).

Study Reveals Positive Effects of Physical Activity Programs for High School Youths

A 2011 study by Fuller, Sabiston, Karp Barrett and O'Laughlin supports the importance of physical activities in schools in the United States. The study employed a weekly checklist of 808 participants to determine data gathered on physical activity in the schools' intramural and extramural activities.

The study found the following from its data and research:

1. Schools should include intramural sports and physical activities to provide opportunities for students to be physically active.
2. The implementation of intramural sport opportunities may influence opportunities for students to become physically active during their transition to adulthood.
3. Even though students may not participate in intramural sports, the fact that a secondary school provides such a program, may lead to positive attitudes toward physical activity.
4. This type of activity support can lead to increases in physical activity behavior within and outside the school.
5. Compared to intramural and physical activity programs, extramural sport programs do not appear to increase phys-

ical activity because extramural does not involve numbers of students and also they involve elite athletes.

Although this represents only one study, "school administrators, teachers and coaches may want to consider these findings when making curricular and programmatic decisions related to increasing adolescent physical activity" (*Journal of School Health*, 81 (8), 449–454. Fuller D., Sabiston, C., Karp, I., Barnett, T, and O'Loughlin, J. 2011).

The High Cost of Community Colleges

Terry Stoops, director of educational studies at the John Locke Foundation, reports the high cost of remediation at community college. Stoops reports that Scott Ralls, president of the N.C. Community College System, reveals that North Carolina spends $90 million a year "to provide remedial courses for its students." Regarding the high cost, Ralls reports that $30 million is used to offer remedial courses to the graduates of recent public schools (*eSchool News*, Oct. 2, 2011). Statewide nearly 40 percent of the recent public school graduates enrolled in remedial English courses and one in four students required a remedial reading course. 93 percent of the students from a highly rated high school enrolled in a remedial reading course. Education leaders in North Carolina have a plan to remedy the problem by:

- Initiating an effort to align and strengthen college readiness and testing standards between the secondary and post-secondary levels.
- Concentrate on policies and procedures to help high school graduates be successful in any post-graduate endeavors (*News & Record*, Oct. 2, 2011).

Chapter 13

Facebook, Twitter and YouTube, Oh My!

JF:

I must admit that I am somewhat of a dinosaur when it comes to technology. In 2002, I still had my tests on an Apple II GS with a dot matrix printer. I held on to my pager (not even a two-way) until 2004, and didn't upgrade my phone to a Blackberry until 2008—I surrendered to the iPhone in 2012. And yes, like so many of my generation, I can't believe how I got along all those years without being able to text—I do it fairly well now, and it does make it very easy to communicate with my entire golf team—instantly. As many of you know all too well, the phone/smartphone is like a new extremity to today's generation of students and trying to figuratively pry it out of their hands for a 55 minute class can be a daunting task, or a real pain in the rear. Nevertheless, as my wife has told me so often, we need to meet our students where they are, and where they are is linked to technology, specifically the connectivity of their technology to their friends and their experiences. I had no knowledge of My Space or Facebook, and I'm kind of glad that I didn't really begin to experience the Facebook phenomena until they seemed to "win the war" to dominate social networking. I guess you have to be patient—just like VHS beat out the Beta Max, Blu Ray beat out HD DVD and now Facebook has apparently beat out MySpace. I do have a Twitter account—but I don't tweet. I just follow a few groups and folks that I like, and while I don't have an official posting on You Tube, my little dog Pearl does have a video — "The Pearl Twirl" (how narcissistic is that?) — I know that LinkedIn is a powerful tool for business people to network, but that doesn't affect our 15–17 year olds very much. My students appear to LOVE Twitter, use Facebook somewhat, but not as often, can't wait to see a new "viral" YouTube video and are into InstaGram.

I really had no earthly idea what Facebook was all about, and the enormous power potential of the darn thing until I "signed on." I swear it wasn't but a couple of days until I had a friend request from a student I had back in the mid-1980s. To read their comments about what they were doing and how much they had enjoyed my class was to have one of Abraham Maslow's Peak Experiences. This was like "Chicken Soup for the Teacher's Soul." I always loved it when former students would come back to visit — particularly during a class — and would tell my students that the best thing about teaching was when students came back to see you. But now, a former student that lives in Florida can give me a shout on Facebook without coming by school. I always knew in my heart that they wouldn't come back unless they cared, and that you had made a difference at some level for them. Please don't ever forget that. Teachers touch lives and make differences that they may never know about. And don't forget that it is NEVER too late to tell someone that they made a difference in your life. This, to me, is the absolute magic of Facebook. The joy I have experienced from getting the positive feedback from former students has brought back great memories and many a tear. I know I am telling you what many of you already know, but this idea of being connected in a social network that makes communication and sharing so easy is way too cool to pass up. If you haven't experienced this yet, take a chance and log in to Facebook and make some connections — especially if some of your old teachers are on it. It makes a huge difference to know that someone is thinking of you — especially a former student. I have told my students that the day after they graduate, if you "friend" me, I would be happy to accept, and they do. My mother-in-law laughs in June when I start to get a crop of new friends, but the way I see it, if the kids appreciated being with you and want to stay connected I'm all for it. Does connecting on a social network have limitations and potential personal and professional risks—of course—but just as a beer commercial asks you to drink responsibly, can't you Facebook responsibly? Let's be honest, NOTHING on the internet is totally safe and secure, so you have to choose your friends wisely and understand what you post could come back to bite you in the butt. Our school board recently decided to develop a social networking policy and specifically a Facebook policy. We are not to "friend" current students and are discouraged to "friend" parents. A local system in an adjacent county is even considering banning teacher from texting students. While I would not routinely text a student, I do utilize texting to communicate with my golf team when I need to let them all know something. It is quick, easy and I know they check it. Again, responsibility and common sense should rule the day. If someone is doing something inappropriate, discipline them—just like you would a student.

In my system, we are allowed to have a Facebook site for an individual class allow students to "like" it in order to get assignments, etc. that might be posted. In addition, our school system has a site that they encourage the community to "like." Universities have been developing acceptable use policies for social media and the University of North Carolina has one specifically designed for athletics. In fact our school system, like so many other entities has links to Facebook, Twitter, LinkedIn and YouTube. Anything to get the message out—and in today's "mediacentric" society, that makes sense.

Of course there are downsides to social media and instantaneous messaging. We hear stories about "flash mobs" getting out of control in different cities, and the potential for libelous posts on any network exists. With regard to my students, the major problem that I have observed relates to the age old "he said, she said" rumor mill that students have always dealt with and that leads to many conflicts in classrooms and schools. The problem now is that things get out of control really quickly thanks to technology. Whether it is actually social media, or a network of text messages, these problems can go viral instantly. Social media is really in its infancy, evolving and growing. We, too, are evolving with this ever-changing technological environment.

HA:

Social Media Concerns

I became interested in the social media that involved Facebook and Twitter when I had the opportunity to teach juniors and seniors in an outstanding secondary school. I became interested in Joe Franks' belief in the value of technology to keep up with his former students. For Joe, the contact with his former students and colleagues is an exciting innovation that he supports.

Because of my newsletter *From the Gym to the Jury*, I had access to some educators who cautioned teachers, administrators, students and parents about some important guidelines to prevent problems linked to the new technology. In the class at a local high school, I had the opportunity to use my network to get outstanding people to speak to our two classes of 25 students each. Tom Walter, the head baseball coach at Wake Forest University, was one of the first guest speakers. Tom received national attention when he donated one of his kidneys to save the life of a freshman student-athlete. At the end of his inspirational talk, Tom Walter discussed college recruiting that had an important impact on all 50 students. Walter told the students that, as Wake Forest's baseball coach, he had a list of 5,000 potential recruits. He explained that he and his coaches responded to every student's inquiry and interest in obtaining a baseball scholarship. He explained how he evaluated each request to 200 prospects. He cautioned the classes to never put anything on Facebook that could cause them problems. Problems, for example that Facebook could use forever because pictures and things written on Facebook belonged to them forever. He told the students that he and his coaches sort out students who had negative pictures and comments that alerted the university that these students were not potential students for his program and that of the university. Gene Banks, an All-American at Duke University and an NBA star, reinforced Walter's presentation. Two-thirds of our speakers, including the agent for Jersey Shore's Snookie, all emphasized the same message. We believe that these guest speakers performed a valuable lesson for students who had no idea that the things they put a Facebook and Twitter could prevent them from college admissions and job opportunities.

In a January, 2012 *eSchool News* conducted a study by the Pew Research Center's Internet and American Life Project. The study revealed that 69 percent of teenagers who use social networking sites believe that "their peers are mostly kind to each other on such sites, but 88 percent say they have witnessed people being mean or cruel on the sites, and 15 percent say they have been the target of mean or cruel behavior themselves."

The study also found that ninety-five percent of U.S. teens, ages 12–17 are online and react in a variety of ways such as:

- 90 percent of teen social media users have ignored the mean behavior they have witnessed on a social network site.
- 90 percent say they have personally defended a victim of meanness and cruelty.
- 79 percent say they have told someone to stop their mean behavior.
- 21 percent say they have personally joined in on the harassment of others on a social network site.

Amanda Lenhart, one of the study's authors, said that the teens who use the social network report that they have both positive and negative experiences from social networking. Lenhart concludes that "One in five said their profile is partially private, while 17 percent say their most-used profile is fully public" (*eSchool News*, January 2012). In another study that was anonymous, more than half of high school seniors "admit that they text or email when driving." Almost 48 percent of high school juniors said that they also texted while driving (*News-Record*, June 8, 2012).

The Centers for Disease Control released the survey and reported that "a typical teen sends and receives about 100 text messages a day." The survey did not discuss whether the car was stopped or in motion.

One of the outcomes in today's technology-driven society is that litigation in social networking has increased as never before. For example:

A middle school principal in northeastern Pennsylvania was shocked to see his picture online. Along with his photo was the following description of him as a "hairy sex addict" and a "pervert" who liked "hitting on students" in his office (*News-Record*, January 2012).

A high school principal in a school north of Pittsburgh saw a MySpace profile of himself that called him a "whore, a big fag, and a drug user." A principal in West Virginia found that a student had created a website to mock another girl as a "slut" with herpes. All three of the students described above were suspended from their schools. All three filed lawsuits arguing that their First Amendment rights were violated because they used their home computers. In the Pennsylvania cases, the students won their case (*McClatchy News Service*, January 16, 2012).

The United States Supreme Court will consider the issues that involve "the rights of students to freely use their own computers and the authority of school officials to prevent online harassment of other students and staff" (*News & Record*, January, 2012).

School officials, as well as parents and students are eager to find what they can do or not do regarding social networking.

20 Athletes Suspended for Facebook Picture

20 high school athletes were disciplined when school authorities saw their pictures on Facebook at a party where they were drinking alcohol. The party was on the weekend at a student's house.

For taking part in the party, the students violated the school's athletic code of conduct. The students were not able to participate in 20 percent of the scheduled football games. In addition, they were assigned to attend substance abuse counseling. The school superintendent Dave Larson said, "This happened off school grounds, during non-school hours, in a private home of a student, so it's a different context if it's a school-supervised event" (*Daily Herald*, Sept. 27, 2012).

Students Can Be Victims or Villains Online

In North Carolina, the state legislative passed legislation that became "a new law that took effect November 1, 2012." The intent of the law "aims to protect teachers and other school employees from cyber-bullying by students. The new law "makes it a misdemeanor punishable by up to 60 days in jail and a $1,000 fine for students to use almost any form of electronic communications to intimidate or torment a school employee" (*News & Record*, Oct. 3, 2012).

The new law illustrates the challenge social media presents to school officials and parents who seek to enforce standards of moral conduct and still preserve "free speech and traditional privacy safeguards." It appears that the legislators want to insulate school employees from "torment" by a student. Critics of the new law raise serious questions such as:

- It can be difficult to track the source of electronic communication.
- It makes certain actions by students unlawful, but what about people who are not students?
- Can a law make certain actions by a student not be a violation by people who are not students?
- Some of the offenses listed are difficult to see as crimes.

The American Civil Liberties Union (ACLU) believes there is a better way to deal with students than pressing charges. ACLU opposes criminalizing speech. The question is raised if you can apply the law to 18- or 19-year-old students, can it apply to adults as well? The law as written is a dilemma because "We want to protect our teachers who don't deserve cyber-taunting by ill-mannered little brats. But the law doesn't get all the details right." Finally, Doug Clark concludes:

> This is a tough arena for legislation and law-enforcement. The technology is racing ahead. It creates an untamed Wild West, where kids are often victims but can be villains too. Where children are concerned, it's more im-

portant to protect them than to prosecute them (*News & Record*, Oct. 3, 2012).

In all probability, the questions raised by the new law will eventually be settled by judicial fiat.

Survey Reveals Teen's Social Media Experiences

A January, 2012 survey reveals 69 percent of teenagers report that social media finds teens kind to each other. However, 88 percent say they have witnessed people being mean and cruel to each other. Also 51 percent say they have been the target of cruel behavior against them. As of January, 2012, teens reported that 95 percent, ages 12–17 are not online and 80 percent of online teams are users of social media (*eSchool News*, January, 2012).

Using Social Media with Your Athletes

Amy Moline, CMAA, is the athletic and recreation director for U-32 High School in Montepelier, Vermont. She conducts workshops that focus on using e-mail, Twitter, Facebook, and texting involving athletic constituents. She notes that these various methods are valuable with a school's attempt to communicate effectively with its constituents. Molina predicts that social media is the wave of the future and the importance of using this technology appropriately (*Interscholastic Athletic Administration*, Spring 2012). She makes several important guidelines that athletic directors and coaches need to follow such as:

1. Keep your coach hat on at all times. If you wouldn't say it to a kid in front of his parents, don't say it online or in a text. You should never use a text or Facebook page to discuss personal topics that do not relate to your team.
2. Consider setting up a professional Facebook page that is only used for communicating with your team. Do not "friend"

any other people except for team members. Or consider creating a "fan" page for your team so that athletes can't access your personal Facebook site.

3. Keep conversations professional and on task when e-mailing, texting or communicating through social media. Announcing that practice is cancelled is appropriate, and commenting on a great effort can be motivational. Scolding a player or commenting on his or her family picnic photos is off-base. Always maintain the same personal boundaries that exist for in-person conversations.

4. Keep your Facebook page and interactions "G-Rated." Party photos with alcohol or shots of you wearing questionable attire might be fun when communicating with adult friends but those things should not be visible to school-aged players. Inappropriate language should also not be used on your page.

5. Your personal and/or your team page should only relate to your team and nothing should be on that page that you would not proudly display to co-workers or of the principals consider "friending" parents of your players so that they can see what is going on your team page.

6. Be aware of your private settings. A setting of "Friends Only" prevents friends of your players from accessing your page. Also if your friends allow generous access to their pages, consider not "friending" players so that they can't find information out by looking at other pages.

7. Check for any state or district policies on the use of social media by school personnel. Some states and schools have legal restrictions in place limiting school personal use of social media (*Interscholastic Athletic Administration*, Spring 2012).

The advice by Amy Molina is helpful to all school programs, not just athletics.

Social Media Plays Bigger Role in Collegiate Athletics

Duke's associate head basketball coach, Steve Wojciechowski, has a following of 18,000 on Twitter. He has a hashtag called "duke-facts" that goes to the 18,000 who follow him on Twitter. Wojciechowski used to contact recruits by telephone but favors today's use of tweets to keep informed of his recruits. He notes that:

> Nowadays, the way the world communicates is so much broader than the (telephone). Social media is a large part of that, especially for the youngest generation.

If a staff member does not "use Twitter or some form, you will get left behind." Dave Telep, ESPN recruiting analyst, believes Twitter is very important. He writes that "This business is based on relationships and information. If you are not using Twitter to form relationships and gather information, somebody needs to welcome you to 2012." Telep said that a NBA general manager poses as a blond on Twitter just to see what reaction he gets with potential players. He believes it gives you the opportunity to "pull back the curtain on the kids they are following. If you are not using it, he says you are in the minority" (*News-Record*, July 30, 2012).

Twitter Problems in Olympics

Guy Adams, a correspondent for a British newspaper, encouraged his readers on Twitter to complain about the networks' coverage. Adams, based in Los Angeles, inadvertently included the email and address of the Olympic president in his Twitter. When Adams checked his Twitter account he found that his Twitter account had been cancelled because of his tweet.

More Trouble on Twitter

Gian Gilli, head of the Swiss Olympic delegation, sent a Swiss soccer player home because she made "insulting remarks about the South Korean soccer team." Gilli found Michel Morganella's tweet "insulting and discriminatory." Gilli said that the remarks "contradict the Olympic charter."

Many participants in the 2012 London Olympics were heavily involved in tweeting. Kobe Bryant and LeBron James had millions of followers on their Twitter pages. Both enjoy tweeting with the millions who follow their tweets. However, despite its popularity, care should be taken to avoid suspensions such as the two described here.

NOTE: U.S. Women's Soccer Goalie, Hope Solo created controversy when she criticized NBC analyst Brandi Chastain for her negative comments about the present U.S. Soccer Team. Solo did not apologize for her outburst on Twitter (*News & Record*, July 31, 2012).

New Missouri Law Is the First in the Nation

Missouri passed the first law regarding the prohibition of school personnel using social media for school personnel to "friend" current and former students who are 18 years old or younger, and have not graduated. The law says "that teachers cannot use e-mail, websites, or work-related social media pages to connect with underage students who are not accessible by administrators and parents/legal guardians."

The law goes into effect in 2012–2013. It specifies that: "teachers cannot establish, maintain or use a work-related website that allows exclusive access with a current or former student" (*eSchool News*, September 11, 2011).

The new Missouri law has touched a nerve nationally and many believe there will be a "copy cat effect" among other states. Many teachers feel that the new law is "an assault on the free speech rights of students and staff." Others express concern that the new law is a "step backwards and a missed opportunity to educate students using new and relevant communication tools."

Nora Carr is the chief of staff for North Carolina's Guilford County Schools. Carr sums up her article on the Missouri law when she concludes:

> The thorny issues posed by such free speech cases by
> an Eighth Circuit court, said these cases present diffi-

cult issues for the court required to protect First Amendment values, while they must be sensitive to the need for a safe-school environment (*eSchool News*, September 2011).

As someone who has been active in reviewing court cases in the field of education and sport law and risk management, I believe there will be considerable issues regarding the use of social media in the public and private schools. It will, in all probability, be controversial and in many instances prompt litigation among those who agree with its value in the educational process to those opposed to ADA compliance and Title IX. And they will develop guidelines for the social media, defining solutions for its use.

It is appropriate in my opinion to look at several cases regarding the use of social media. As previously noted, the United States Supreme Court will consider the issues that involve "The rights of students to freely use their own computers and the authority of school officials to prevent online harassment of other students and staff" (*News-Record*, January 2010).

School officials, as well as parents and students are eager to find what they can do or not do regarding social networking.

Social Media

Along with the benefits and potential for increased communication, a word of caution is due. A North Carolina Court of Appeals ruled that "false statements posted on Facebook and a political website libeled a judge and should be heard by a jury for determination of actual malice and damages" (*News & Record*, May 4, 2012).

A judge who was running for re-election endorsed another judge. An unpaid strategist for another candidate running for the same seat wrote on Facebook that the judge was violating the Code of Judicial Conduct when she campaigned for another judge. When the strategist was told that he was wrong and a judge running for an election could endorse another candidate, the media strategist apologized for his error and then repeated his objection on Facebook by claiming it as his opinion.

The N.C. Court of Appeals disagreed and held that "An individual cannot preface an otherwise defamatory statement with in my opinion and claim immunity from liability."

The court agreed that Americans should be free to criticize public officials, but concluded that it's different, though, when a writer knows exactly what the facts are yet purposely hides or misrepresents them and publishes a groundless opinion anyway. Once again, bloggers should take note that they can be held accountable for what they put online (*News & Record*, Sept. 2012).

Many reviewers of the first presidential debate between President Obama and Mitt Romney expressed their opinion of the candidates and their attempt to persuade voters to support their candidacy. Scott Talan, an assistant professor of communications at American University, who studies social media and politics said:

> People still use old media to watch the debates, but they use social networks to have influence, voice opinions and be involved (*News & Record*, Oct. 5, 2012).

Twitter reported that the debate "had been the most tweeted event in U.S. history with 11.1 million comments" (*News & Record*, Oct. 5, 2012).

"The new world of social media illustrates the challenge presents to school administrators, parents, and others seeking to enforce basic standards of moral conduct, shield children from filth and sexual come-ons, and yet preserve free speech and traditional privacy safeguards" (*News & Record*, Oct. 1, 2012).

Chapter 14

The 6 Cs for the 21st Century

HA:

Patrick Bassett, former chief executive of the National Association of Independent Schools (NAIS), travels world-wide to review education programs abroad. He is recognized as a world-wide expert with deep experience in private, independent schools. Bassett has made presentations on all aspects of education and his many presentations are carefully followed internationally. Bassett's advice on what is necessary to meet the needs of those who want to make a difference in education and life is well-received virtually everywhere. His recommendations for the best practices in education for the 21st century follow:

1. Creativity—a concerted emphasis should be made to utilize the right brain. Many foreign countries have emphasized the linear and focus on the left brain. Today, Asian countries emphasize the development of the right brain to achieve creativity by students. The United States, according to Bassett, needs to make a calculated effort to expand its practices to put a greater premium on the right brain and creativity.

2. Character—for years, many educators felt the need to continue to develop programs of character development called Civics. However, these courses primarily emphasized government. Today, character education plays an increasingly important role in education in our schools. These efforts include integrity, ethical behav-

ior and earnest concern for others. They are the "common wheel" of the new program.

3. Critical Thinking—on the collegiate level most have included critical thinking as a requirement in all courses. Critical thinking challenges the status quo in the curriculum. Its purpose is to create new knowledge and to avoid teaching only to the test.

4. Communication—developing the ability to speak and write clearly. A new ability, learning to listen, is an important quality often overlooked.

5. Cosmopolitanism—a curriculum that is cross-cultural and global. This trend is growing and more schools are investing time and finances to make sure it becomes an important element in U.S. education.

6. Collaboration—develop the capacity to work together, to share knowledge as never before. An example of this "C" occurs when a class of 20 students break into four groups with five in each group. Each group selects an area to research in various areas: medicine, government, law, economics, etc. The group shares their research within the group and then meets with the other four groups to become aware of others research. Sidwell Friend in Washington, D.C. works diligently on collaboration in middle school. One of their classes corresponds with a Chinese class in China. Both programs share information on a regular basis and report exciting sharing of information.

For information on the 6 "Cs", go to NAIS.org.

Chapter 15

Sidwell Friends School: Innovative Approaches to Education in the 21st Century

HA:

In a discussion with Bruce Stewart, the former headmaster at Sidwell Friends, we learned that several policies and practices are in concert with our experiences on both the high school and college levels. In an August, 2012 discussion, Stewart pointed out several outstanding practices which are in concert with our beliefs.

- Consider encouraging students to become fluent in a second language. In China and other countries, students become fluent in English, almost from the start of school. Like China, many other countries encourage and require their students to become fluent in a second language. In most, English is the choice. Stewart noted that a Volkswagon franchise recently opened in Chattanooga, Tennessee. As a result, 30+ German students enrolled in the community's schools. Many American students quickly picked up the study of German and the German students promptly became fluent in English. Cross-disciplinary studies became popular and the German students enrolled in courses such as U.S. history, U.S. literature, American culture and economics.

- Skyping — U.S. students connect with other countries in courses such as Physics and Mathematics. International students interact with U.S. students in a range of social sciences and humanities offerings.
- At Guilford College, interdisciplinary courses were offered for many years. My Legal Issues in Sport course regularly had 40 or more students and it was typical to have many from Japan, Scotland and other international communities. Also, we had majors as diverse as Biology, Mathematics, Foreign Languages, Economics, Sociology and Psychology.
- Overseas Study — regularly for one semester and up to one full year. Sidwell would not charge these students for their semester or year but let parents use the Sidwell cost to pay for the semester or year abroad.
- Teamwork is encouraged at Sidwell as students are routinely encouraged to get involved in student government, clubs, athletics, the arts and community service.
- Sidwell pointed to Washington International School where fluency in a second language is required.
- Sidwell stresses, as we all should, co-curricular and interdisciplinary activities for all students.
- Emphasis is placed on Experiential Learning where middle school students plant gardens and learn about all facets of the growing process. Only organic food is served in the school cafeteria, and SFS tries not to purchase food grown more than 100 miles from campus. Students learn the how and why of food growth and nutrition.
- Technology is very important. Students use technologies in their courses, and they do so from lower school on. Recently, I worked with a high school student to develop power points to include in a forthcoming book. I asked her how she became so proficient in these techniques and she answered, "I started in the fourth grade and continued with it all through high school." Not only does Sidwell encourage the use of technology, but it teaches students how to protect themselves and others when they employ it.

- LEED values are emphasized at the school (L—Leadership, E—Environment, E—Energy, D—Design). Most buildings seek to comply with LEED criteria throughout. The LEED program has the following rating levels: Platinum, Gold, Silver, and Bronze. A building can be LEED certified if it embraces the LEED Engineering, Construction and Architecture requirements.
- Put LEED curriculum in the classroom. For example, use the classroom to explore the feasibility of a green roof at a school. The class can examine all facets of being LEED green—the cost, why, how, expenses and the value.
- Every teacher is expected to discuss and include Ethics in every course.
- Sidwell leaders have been mindful of Finland's policies and practices in education. There teachers must finish high in their graduating classes. Their jobs pay extremely well and hold genuine prestige.
- As an independent school, Sidwell focuses on hiring outstanding people who may not have teaching certification. SFS believes that public schools in the United States can be encumbered by certification requirements that are too rigid. Several examples are given:
  a. An attorney who was an expert in Constitutional law and practiced before a number of high courts in the nation's capitol became an exceptional high school history teacher.
  b. An attorney who wanted to teach rather them practice law. Without certification she became an excellent middle school Mathematics teacher.
- Hiring capable and outstanding individuals to teach, who may lack standard certification, can be a definite plus. (At Guilford College this practice attracted many talented adjunct professors for years. Those intellectually well-qualified practitioners greatly enhanced the college's academic program for years.)
- Sidwell utilizes a somewhat unique hiring policy. They consider the demographics of the population in the greater Washington, D.C. area, and that diversity is the key in their hiring, including consideration of:

a. Age
b. Race
c. Religion
d. Life style
e. Gender
f. Intellectual depth
g. Globalism
h. Career experience
i. Passion for teaching field
j. Care for students
k. Moral compass
l. Commitment to institutional mission

- When Sidwell considers hiring a teacher or staff member they ask for references, but routinely contact others whose names are not given by the prospective teacher. Sidwell then develops a team to review the credentials to evaluate several class presentations by the prospective teacher. Peer and student reviews are sought and well considered.
- Public speaking and debate are important but debate is limited in many schools today. Sidwell urges teachers to have considerable dialogue in class and in an extracurricular activity. Faculty give attention to spontaneous speaking and oral presentations in class.
- Teach students the ability to civilly disagree with or challenge anything discussed in class. This is a needed skill and students must learn it while being respectful of others.
- Listening to students is a valuable skill. When a student approached Bruce Stewart, he reminded the Headmaster that they had not had a single snow day that year. Stewart made the following Wednesday a "SNOW DAY" much to the approval of students, parents and colleagues. In addition, the Headmaster welcomed other colleague concerns, but did not necessarily grant or comply with every request. When some community members wanted to cut the number of classes (about 180), they were told that this was one request that could not be granted.

- Homework Reversal—Sidwell sometimes replaced traditional homework by having students work on conventional class material online at night in their homes. The next day they were able to discuss the online lessons. This change of the traditional instructional cycle was every popular and quite effective.
- Technology—Bernie Noe, a talented teacher and administrator at Sidwell, moved to Seattle, Washington to become Headmaster in Lakeside, a district in Seattle. There, he formed a national coalition of independent schools that each agreed to offer a certain number of exceptional online classes that could be taken by students from any member institution. The offerings are excellent and challenging, and they have been very well received. The effort represents a truly cutting edge use of technology and it is a wonderful example of institutional cooperation that benefits everyone involved.
- Evaluation of Teachers—every new teacher comes with the full understanding that their work will be carefully reviewed. The evaluation process is conducted by principals, academic deans, deans of students, department chairs, counselors and other faculty, as well as having select input from students and parents.

Sidwell Friends believes that feedback from students and parents is extremely helpful and extremely important, but it is reviewed with appropriate care and concern. As a result of the evaluation by such a diverse group, faculty can be supported, applauded and celebrated, but they can also be assisted with growth and need changes. Considerable school resources are directed toward faculty professional development, and it is a key part of the school culture to be a continuing learner. Some teachers are not retained while others are placed on probation. Stewart feels that such an annual review is necessary.

Patrick Bassett observes that independent schools often have more opportunities and resources than many public schools. For example, there are numerous Quaker schools around the country that share information with each other about trends in contemporary education. Many colleges and universities around the United States are recruiting overseas to add to the diversity of their communities through direct and indirect global learning. Numerous universities have joined together to send recruiters to visit secondary schools in various countries. One such example is Appalachian State University, a public university in the mountains of North Carolina. The school has recruited in dozens of schools in China, with the goal of bringing talented Asian students to the Boone campus. In the past, a large number of schools elected to send their students to other countries to have a global learning experience. Today, many universities are bringing international students to the United States to undertake their undergraduate and graduate degrees, and while this approach greatly enhances the global perspective for them, it also does so for every American student.

Chapter 16

A Look to the Future

Annie Clement[*]:

It is the year 2020, less than ten years from today. If you view the world as an optimist, you are vacationing in space. The space station has replaced Disney World as the number one vacation destination for family fun. If you are a pessimist, you are fleeing your home and/or the country because of terrorist activities, an economic crisis, a failure of municipal infrastructure, or hazardous weather conditions. All these events could occur in the year 2020. The optimist and the pessimist are playing with predictions, the generation of ideas about the future. And what are the chances of a prediction becoming reality? Let's look at a few past predictions. In August 1948, *Science Digest* reported that landing and moving around on the moon would offer so many serious problems for human beings that it would take science another 200 years to lick them. Neil Armstrong walked on the moon on July 20, 1969—less than thirty years later. And when television first appeared, some predicted that after about six months, people would tire of staring at a box every evening. Today, watching television is a major pastime. In 1990, Clement predicted that office buildings would have health spas, that hospital wellness centers would open their doors to the public, and that robots would be the tennis partners of choice

---

* Ph.D, J.D., University of New Mexico Sports Administration Faculty member.

by the year 2000 (Parks & Zanger, 1990). Health spas and hospital wellness centers flourished in the 1990s. Robotic tennis partners never became reality. However, "Japanese scientists have invented a soccer playing robot called VisiON; they claim a team of such robots will win the World Cup by 2050" (Brown, 2006, pp. 51–52).

Daydreaming Is Thinking

Contemplating the future is a creative venture that challenges the imagination and frees the mind to dream. It forces one to ignore concerns of daily life; it makes daydreaming legitimate. We tend to clutter our time with tasks that demand that work hours produce something for which we are accountable. We fail to daydream and use our imagination for the joy of thinking. Seldom do we engage in lateral thinking, the transfer of known ideas to solve new problems (DeBono, 1970). Remember that as a "future sport manager, you are limited only by the extent of your imagination" (Parks & Zanger, 1990, p. 257). The purpose of this chapter is to enable the reader to put contemporary concerns aside and follow futurists toward the years 2020, 2030, and 2050.

The Journey

In 1980, Toffler (1980) explained the impending crisis in our country as the death of industrialism and the rise of a new civilization, a civilization he called "the third wave," or "the information age." Waldrop (1992) states that the "linear, reductionist thinking that has dominated science and research since the time of Newton is no longer capable of addressing modern work problems" (p. 13). He sees today's systems as spontaneous, disorderly, and alive. Waldrop (1992) believes: "[C]omplex systems have somehow acquired the ability to bring order and chaos into a special kind of balance. This balance point — often called the edge of chaos — is where the components of a system never quite lock into place, and yet never quite dissolve into turbulence.... The edge of chaos is where life has enough stability to sustain itself and enough creativity to deserve the name of life" (p. 12). Pink (2005) suggests that we are in a period of movement from the Information Age to the Conceptual Age. He states: "We are moving from an economy and a society built on the logical, linear, computer-like capabilities of the Information Age to an economy and a society built on the inventive, empathic, big-picture capabilities of what's rising in its place, the Conceptual Age" (p. 2). Aburdene (2005) describes society's massive change as a move from the information age or economy to social responsibility. She envisions the demise of "business as usual" to the birth of Conscious Capitalism. "Creativity and innovation are the name of the game" (p. xv). For Aburdene (2005), "consciousness, the prime ingredient in creativity, represents a higher intelligence than the mind" (p. xvi). Aburdene's focus on spirituality, the greatest mega-trend of contemporary society, is driven by the current threat of manmade and natural disasters or terrorism, contemporary wars, and lost savings. Her purpose is to dispel the notion "that free enterprise is rooted in greed" (p. xxii). She goes on to state: "Conscious Capitalism isn't altruism, either; it relies instead on the wisdom of enlightened self interest" (p. xxii). She disagrees with the idea that the sole purpose of a for-profit business is to make money for the shareholders. Her thesis is that the business, while trying to make a profit, must be concerned with the needs of society. In addition, Aburdene suggests that many of the recent illegal actions of major businesses were prompted by the need of executives to find more ways of unscrupulously improving shareholders investments. Had CEOs held a sense of corporate social responsibility, these problems would not have occurred.

Change

Our only guarantee for the future is that things will change, change rapidly, and change continuously. What changes are we currently experiencing? Service organizations have replaced the steel and coal industries; as a result, intellect or knowledge possessed by the work force has replaced the physical labor required of those who worked in the past. People, capable of planning, thinking, and implementing, have become our primary economic asset. People are important to the world economy; they are more im-

portant than buildings and factories. Ideas and the resolution of
complex problems, rather than the speed in which an object can be
manufactured, commands success today and will command success in the 2020 economy. Reorganization and reconfiguration of
existing technologies and ideas, many that have been invented and
patented but have not been mainstreamed, will be used by a wide
range of consumers. Planning, as a concept, will take on new meaning. We will look to the future attempting to accurately predict
events, needs, and services essential to success in that future. Less
time will be dedicated to analyzing the success of earlier achievements, and greater effort will be placed on creating alternate futures. While history will continue to be cherished and used to
examine events in the context of success and failure, future thinking will guide the growth and development of our businesses. How
will you and I know that it is 2020? Technology will have so taken
over our daily needs that a person will rise to a breakfast prepared
by an appliance and live in a home, office, transportation vehicle,
and other environment preprogrammed to personal specifications.
When the cost of the refrigerator that inventories food and orders
replacements has come within the reach of the masses, few grocery
stores, as we know them today, will exist. Massive food warehouses
will satisfy our needs for groceries; a few stores will be available to
those who consider shopping a hobby. Household chores and the
cleaning of our dwellings will be the job of programmed appliances
and robots. Engineer futurists envision that these appliances will or-
chestrate our daily requirements and cater to our needs, while bi-
ologists believe that chemical changes and other changes in the air
will be the answer to cleaning. Although not all of the processes
are clear, we will have eliminated general household chores. Our
homes will have comprehensive work environments for each in-
habitant, thus making them much larger than they are today. In a
paperless, or near paperless, society, the space once dedicated to
libraries will be comfort zones for effective work and leisure. Computers will be small and often worn as jewelry. We will be in the
beginning of the genetic revolution. Parents will determine their
offspring's genetic makeup prior to birth. As a result, a coach, for
example, may face serious problems with parents whose children

were engineered to be outstanding athletes when the coach fails to see the child as an accomplished performer.

Research Charting the Course of Predictions for the Years 2020, 2030 and 2050

Research dictating societal change will be addressed in this section—which will focus on energy, health and longevity, food, life style, manmade and natural disasters, literacy, and education and employment. Emphasis will be placed on sport, leisure, and tourism. Globalization, technology, and creativity will influence these topics and will propel us into the future.

Energy

Energy, or power, is a main source of our economy. Societies' needs for transportation, air conditioning and heat, electricity, and other forms of energy are beyond necessity; many feel they could not survive without them. In order to provide these services in the future, new sources of energy will be identified and developed. Advancement toward that goal can be seen in the projects at Fraunhofer Institute in Germany and in Hanoi University of Technology that convert rice husks into electricity (Tomorrow in Brief, 2007; Fraunhofer Institute, http://www.fraunhofer.de). At the same time researchers at Florida Atlantic University in Boca Raton, Florida, are harnessing the Gulf Stream as a source of power to generate electricity (Environment, 2007). Recently, light fixtures have seen radical change toward efficiency. The compact fluorescent light is about four times as efficient as an incandescent bulb. The Ostar LED, a mercury-free light that will glow for 60,000 hours, is ready for market, and professionals predict that by 2010, glowing walls lit by sheets of organic light emitting diodes (OLED) will illuminate our homes, businesses, and community facilities (Bright Lights, Big Savings, 2007). Batteries have also changed and are predicted to continue to increase the number of hours of service. Home design and construction professionals will make use of nature's light and energy in future living quarters.

Health and Longevity

Life spans of one hundred to one hundred and twenty years will be reality in the next thirty to fifty years. Genetic engineering, bionics, stem cell science, and pharmacology will enable people to lead productive lives into their 90s and 100s. Zey (2005a, 2005b) calls this change in longevity "super longevity" and defines it as the "radical extension of the human life span accompanied by improved health and vibrancy at all ages" (Zey, 2005a, p. 1). Two factors that will play an important role in longevity are the replacement of body parts, a phenomenon of today's medical environment taken many steps forward, and the replacement of body organs, including lungs. Swansea University in Wales has developed an artificial lung (Tomorrow in Brief, 2007; Swansea University, http://www.swansea. ac.uk). The genetic engineering of children will also play a significant role in the extension of life into the 100s. "Health enhancement rights fueled by the wealth of aging baby boomers and the fusion of nano, bio, IT and neuro innovation, will become a fierce social issue" (Canton, 2006, p. 118).

Food

Diet, exercise, and life style influence health and longevity. Water is a primary concern of contemporary and future societies, since potential shortages are a reality. Efforts by researchers throughout the world to convert salt water to potable water may ease the shortage. Health will be improved through the use of new laser-based technology for detecting food-borne pathogens and through chemical-based technology for killing pathogens on fresh produce—both recent accomplishments of a Purdue University food scientist (Tomorrow in Brief, 2007; http://www.purdue.edu/UNS). Food shortages will be a concern in the United States because of the elimination of vast farm lands. Farms in skyscrapers, according to Despommier (2007), will leave the green fields of the Midwest and move to thirty-story buildings in urban centers. He envisions abandoned buildings in urban areas retrofitted for hydroponics. Irrigation would come from desludged sewage filtered through nonedible barrier plants and zebra mussels, resulting in pristine water. In addition, NASA is currently working on a wide range of products that can be grown indoors for use on Mars and on Earth (Despommier, 2007).

Lifestyle

Lifestyle will undergo the greatest change, as virtual reality is incorporated into daily, leisure, and business activities. For example, most of our household products will be ordered from a wireless television or handheld devices. As soon as the order is placed, money will be deducted from a bank or a special type of account to pay for the order. Some predict that a new form of credit will eliminate cards and bank accounts. Today's problems with privacy, security, and counterfeiting of paper currency will result in a cashless society (Kupetz, 2007). The order will be delivered by a flying drone. Before this chapter goes to press, wireless telephones will have TVs. Shortly, the telephone will begin to control household appliances. Security systems and strategically placed cameras will monitor activities in the homes and workplace. Telephone, television, and the Internet will be fully integrated by 2020. In 2050, roads and highways will no longer exist, as travel will be conducted by helicopter-type vehicles, some controlled by humans and others manipulated by drones or robots. These machines will be stored outdoors or in special housing, with two or three portal landing strips accompanying each living quarter. Today's robots are vacuum cleaners, machines that enter places unavailable to humans, or assembly lines. Tomorrow's robots will serve the evening cocktails, locate the newspaper, input computer data, and alert owners to danger. As space travel becomes popular, people will choose to live on the moon or on space platforms. *Wired*, in July 2007, provided pictures of homes or lunar habitats planned by NASA contractors for living on the moon. The structures will accommodate daytime temperatures of 250 degrees Fahrenheit and nighttime lows of minus 450 degrees Fahrenheit. NASA reports that these homes will be operative by 2020 (Kuang, 2007).

Manmade and Natural Disasters

Among the disasters faced today and projected for the immediate future is the manmade disaster of terrorism. Privacy (or lack of privacy), a national security issue, accompanies many of the terrorism solutions. Another issue is the relationship between terrorism and oil. If the need for oil is substantially reduced, could the threat of terrorism be reduced? The aging of the United State's infrastructures — highways, bridges, power plants, water systems, and so forth — is a potential manmade disaster. Natural disasters such as hurricanes, tornadoes, floods, mountain slides, and fires will cause damage and change. These changes will be geographic, financial, and related to lifestyle. Global warning is predicted to eliminate much of today's Atlantic and Pacific residential coasts. Taxes and insurance may also erode the value of coastal dwellings. Should disasters, manmade or natural, continue at the pace of the recent past, economic structures will change.

Literacy

Futurists predict the end of the written word and the rise of visual culture. Video and video games are the choice of today's youth; newspaper purchases are on the decline. Text messaging is in; written notes are out. Crossman (2004) states that by the year 2050, "talking computers incorporating multisensory, multimodal technology will make written language obsolete and all writing and reading will be replaced by speech and multisensory content, recreating a world wide oral culture" (p. 27). He further believes that the "three Rs — reading, riting and rithmetic — will be replaced by the 4 Cs, critical thinking, creative thinking, computer skills, and calculators." Crossman's (2004) logic for the change to an oral culture is based on four factors he identifies as engines. First, biology and psychology directs us to use speech-based methods. Second, written language is a form of technology, and like all technologies, it can be replaced. Third, youth are rejecting the written word for verbal and visual relationships. Letters are being replaced with telephone calls. And fourth, language and communication barriers will be removed as people will be able to communicate with the 80 percent of adults who are functionally nonliterate (Crossman, 2004). "The voice recognition technology that allows simultaneous translation of spoken language from one language to another is in place. And the software that translates speech into on-screen 3-D sign language is here" (Crossman, 2004, p. 9). These changes will enable all humans to communicate with one another and to enjoy the culture of all parts of the world. The technology, available within the next ten years, will change the course of social interaction around the world. Naisbitt (2006) confirms Crossman's views, stating: "a visual culture is taking over the world" (p. 113). His rationale includes the decline of newspapers, the value of pictures in advertising, upscale design, fashion, architecture and art, music, video and film, the changing role of photography, and the availability of museums. Naisbitt mentions design and creativity as key elements in the economy, thus supporting the view of Pink (2005).

Education and Employment

Although predictions were made that by now schools would no longer exist, these predictions have not occurred. However, elementary schools, middle schools, and high schools have changed radically in delivery systems over the past ten years and are expected to continue to change. Higher education has taken the giant leap in altering the learning environment through online or distance learning. It is anticipated that this higher education model will be the model for all forms of education. Within the immediate future or by 2020, higher education students will acquire all factual knowledge online. However, they will continue to attend interactive seminars to share ideas and sharpen social skills. Elementary schools, middle schools, and high schools will follow the college model but will continue to include face-to-face social interaction. The changes in literacy and technology will enable persons from their early years to their old age to communicate effectively with people all over the world. Computers will translate messages in such a way that no effort will be needed to learn the language of the person with whom you are working. Thus, the potential for a global economy will be in place.

Increased longevity, with the masses living to over 100 years, will be accompanied by changes in careers. The life work sequence of forty to fifty years will change to seventy to eighty years. These changes will enable or require people to plan for four, five, or six different careers during their lifetimes. New skill sets will be necessary for each career and within many of the careers. A difficult change will be the loss of seniority as a value in the workplace, with success based principally on current skill capacity. This change is influenced by the speed with which technology renders work skills obsolete. Employment will be global, with various parts of the world known as the leaders in certain industries. If one wishes to be employed in a particular field, it may require study and employment in the country that specializes in that field. Those changes will create common wage and working conditions across boundaries, thus eliminating today's outsourcing of labor to countries that pay low wages. Project manager specialists will replace many of today's CEOs in the business world; the specialists will hold key roles in business and industry and will be independent contractors. They will move from one business to another while carrying out major projects. Project managers, as a result of technology, will be international. Naisbitt (2006) suggests that as business, industry, and education become global, we will move toward a world government.

Changes in Sport, Leisure, and Global Tourism

International globalization and technology will have a profound effect on sport as we know it today. Naisbitt (2006) notes that today, sport permits the United States to lead in globalization. He credits sport's sharing of talent as being what puts sport way ahead of most other sectors of the United States. "Embedded in the sports model is a preview of what will happen in the economic domain" (p. 174). Team member selection and employment is international. At the same time, nearly all professional sport franchises have a physical presence, playing games and holding championships in countries throughout the world. Individual sport athletes in tennis and golf often study with people around the world, while athletes from all over the world come to America to train and live. The Olympics and regional competitions require sports to use common rules and strategies throughout the world. Television and technology bring new games and contests to the viewer every day. For example, fifteen years ago, the U. S. Olympic basketball team was seen in 180 countries. Chuck Daly, discussing this event in with a reporter in the June 21, 2007 issue of *USA Today*, mentioned that a native of Sudan, Chicago Bulls star and former Duke player Luol Deng, an NBA professional, witnessed the basketball games and switched from soccer to basketball. Recently, the author saw a piece on television introducing cross-country walking as a new fitness activity. Cross-country walking was a popular pastime thirty years ago, when she studied in Norway. In addition, sport has been instrumental in achieving unity throughout the world, even in troubled times.

Visual

Sport and entertainment bridge the gap to the visual future. Although many people who continue to read the newspaper check the sport page carefully and others read concert programs, most sport and entertainment spectator time is spent in the visual culture. Intellectual property knowledge, currently advanced by the sport and entertainment community, will become the model for intellectual property in all visual business sectors.

Fitness

Future sport and physical activity will provide: fitness for everyone, careers in amateur and professional sport, opportunities for individuals of all ages to achieve personal success and to enjoy the social aspects of participation. Sport management personnel will oversee or manage all of these areas. Within each of the physical activity areas, physiologists, biomechanics (skill specialists), medical personnel, athletic trainers, and strategy specialists will play a role in helping people achieve their objectives. Technology has had a tremendous impact on sport at all levels. The computer and sophisticated programs enable coaches to use biomechanical analysis in the coaching of skills and strategies. The same equipment is a must in observing game play and strategy for opponents and team members. Technology has revolutionized stadiums and arenas—from the scoreboard to seating and storage. Games and computer programs have generated considerable revenue for sports figures and agencies and promise to provide new and exciting experiences. Virtual reality sports are big business for participants and spectators. The design of sport programs to meet the needs of people with free time will be the responsibility of the sport management professional. The literature on the future suggests that people will have more free time as a result of reduced work hours per week and reduction in time required for household tasks, personal responsibilities, and education; however, none of the authors consulted for this chapter stated such as fact. If many of the tasks and jobs that consume our time today are eliminated, new recreational, leisure, and spectator activities will need to be designed. These activities will be discussed under the headings "participant" and "spectator."

Participant

Many people within sport believe that the greatest change will be found in society's desire to participate in sport and physical activity. Fitness, prompted by the obesity epidemic of 2000 to 2015, will become a part of everyone's life. The desire for longevity will also fuel the fire for fitness, and business and industry will reward those who remain fit. Fitness centers will exist for people from three years old to over eighty. Participation in team, individual, extreme, and new forms of sport, yet to be named, will exist. Competitive and social experiences will be provided for common skill levels in each sport or activity. Play will resemble the type of play provided today in adult tennis, golf, and skiing. Those wishing to compete at their ultimate personal skill level will have ample opportunity to achieve their goals. Those using sport as a means of meeting people and socializing will have many opportunities to satisfy their desires, while those wishing to engage in human movement for the joy of moving will be offered a full range of activities. Programs to simulate weightlessness will be popular among those planning short- and long-term trips to the moon and the planets circling Earth. Sport specialists will manage massive fitness enterprises designed to measure fitness using medical-stress and space-age technology. Computer-generated personal fitness scores derived from health, nutrition, and genetic composition will be scanned by a computer from a bar code on the nail of the fourth finger of the person's left hand and will be available free of charge to everyone. Facilities or rooms of capsules will house simulation laboratories designed to develop personal human movement basics and sport skills. Camera and movement film streams embedded in the individual learning capsule will enable participants to understand the quality of their over-arm throw or their capacity to move upright after using a commode, whichever skill the person wants to learn. Pictures from the capsule camera will automatically be digitized, sent to a database reference of efficient skill for the movement and the size of the individual, and within seconds, the performer will have a readout of the quality of his or her performance and the next step in improving that performance or in bringing it in line with the perfect form according to principles of anatomy and physics. Therapists and sport skill specialists will be available to guide individual skill development. Those aspiring to game play will receive information as to whether personal skills are beginning, intermediate, advanced, or expert (Clement & Hartman, 1994) and which game-play simulators will provide them with skills specific to a particular sport. Sport and game virtual-reality capsules will simulate position and game play from partner play to small-group play and, finally, to full-team play. Virtual reality will enable the athlete first to mimic his or her role by using rules and strategies; then the performer will actually move in response to those with whom he or she is playing in the virtual world. When the performer has achieved intermediate skill and strategy levels, he or she will leave the learning capsule and enter the gymnasium to begin to play with humans. In competitive sport, capsules will be programmed to simulate real competition. Physical-skill level, nutrition, and genetic background of players will be one of the most guarded secrets and will be covered by contemporary privacy law. Technology will have made this information valuable to opponents. An advantage of the above approach to the acquisition of skill, knowledge of rules, and game play is that the mental components of rules and strategies will be acquired in virtual reality, thus eliminating the overuse injuries that occur among athletes who spend too many hours playing to acquire game knowledge and strategy knowledge. Even though nanomachines will repair and replace joints, tendons, nerves, brain cells, and other body parts, athletes will want to conserve body structure in the hope of remaining competitive in senior events for as long as 125 to 130 years. Swimming and gymnastics will be coveted by the masses these activities will be essential to successful space travel. This assumes that scientists will not have overcome the problems of weightlessness; thus, the space station will necessitate that persons learn to move in a weightless environment. Trampolines and thick bouncing mats will be used to assist people in the first stage of overcoming weightlessness. The practice of underwater aquatic movements taken from water polo and synchronized swimming will enable persons to move efficiently and socially in the space village. Knowledge of placement from indoor soccer, ice hockey, and billiards will assist performers in applying their bodies' force against firm structures as a means of moving in space. Once these skills are acquired, space athletes will attend workshops using discarded astronaut simulators. NordicTrack, Nike, and others who have survived the economic crises will market simulators for home use. The physically challenged person will seldom exist, as technology will have repaired limbs and organs. Mentally challenged persons will be fewer in number than they are today as a result of genetic engineering and the replacement of brain cells. The role of stress, drugs, and other psychological factors in the future is unclear, as is the potential for personal hazards that cannot be identified. All of these changes will have an impact on the human body and personality and could result in problems. Should worst-case scenarios of terrorism play a role in the immediate future, the population will be prepared, physically and psychologically, for disaster. And that preparation will have been accomplished through adventure education—knowing how to function in the wilderness. The acquisition of camping, hiking, climbing, nutrition, and health skills in the wild will be as important as knowing how to effectively brush one's teeth.

Spectator

At the same time, a wide range of sport entertainment will be provided for spectators. With three hundred to five hundred television stations available, networks will be dedicated not only to traditional sports but to dance, synchronized swimming, diving, fencing, and field hockey. This change will open employment to a far greater number of athletes than that which exists today. As schools and colleges began to disappear in 2020, scholastic and collegiate sport in the United States will move to the club model popular in the rest of the world. Special clubs will be established to meet the needs of the much larger population of athletes who will aspire to professional sport as a career. John Sweeney (2007), founder of the University of North Carolina Sports Communication Program identifies ten key trends that will shape the future of the sports industry. The first key trend is branding, with a recognized unifying logo. He points out that the "future belongs not just to those who understand branding, but to those able to achieve the enormous political discipline necessary to make it work" (Sweeney, 2007, p. 35). The second key trend is a need to change the media, while the third trend will be what women's sports will bring to the media. The next trends are the changes that will occur in viewer attention once there are a hundred TV stations: the value of wealth; the replacement of participation by spectatorship, primarily on TV; the influence of environmental change; engineered athletes; global change; and moral connections (Sweeney, 2007). Sweeny has challenged the managers of the amateur and professional sport industry with these words. Branding, along with the elimination of the written word, will place responsibility on tomorrow's sport management professionals to understand and achieve success in the area of preservation through intellectual property law. Leisure and tourism, in conjunction with sport, will make use of the forms of transportation essential to short- and long-term space travel and periods of living on space platforms or villages and the moon. One of the new sports proposed is "dive from space." People will ride a rocket into space, abandon the rocket, and jump or dive from about 60 miles above Earth. The dive will be used as a safety device for persons facing problems while touring outer space and for those who intentionally enter outer space for this new sport. Sophisticated space suits will enable the body to withstand the heat of reentry and will provide oxygen to the diver (Weed, 2007). International travel will be commonplace since people will wish to visit with those with whom they have been communicating for years. Camping and outdoor adventures will become important, as people shed the fear of terrorism but wish to use the well-honed skills acquired for long-term survival in remote areas. Sport managers will play the lead role in the entertainment industry as they meet the needs of spectators and will lead amateur sport organizations in the provision of opportunities for all. The proliferation of television stations will enable the viewer in 2020 to watch only those sports of interest. Viewer selection will drive sports virtually ignored into mainstream entertainment.

Scenarios Specific to the Future
Characteristics of 2020

- Agriculture waste and wind will convert to electricity; all power will be electric or solar.
- Efficient light in homes and offices will be provided by windows and open spaces.
- People will live to 90 to 100 years of age and will work until 70 to 75 years of age.
- Technology, research, fitness, and nutrition will make longevity possible.
- Extended life span will require learning for multiple careers.
- Conversion of salt water to drinking water and laser-based technology for detecting and killing food-borne pathogens will increase longevity.

- Household needs, including groceries and other items, will be ordered from hand-held devices and delivered to homes.
- Vehicles will be created but will not be owned by many.
- Television, telephone, and the Internet will be fully integrated.
- Robots will do general household chores.
- People will be prepared for natural and manmade disasters.
- Cell phones and other social devices will put people in close touch with a small but intimate group of their selection. Families and friends will be able to maintain close contact even though they are miles apart.
- Athletes will use virtual reality for practice and skill development.
- Robots will become practice partners in sport.
- Personal skill levels of the average population will be elevated.
- A high level of fitness will be rewarded by employers.
- An increase in jobs for professional athletes and sport and media communication specialists will occur in a wide range of sports to meet the expansion of television stations.
- International sport competition will increase.
- American sport franchises at home and abroad will be at their peak, with spectators frequently traveling to other parts of the world to see their favorite teams.
- New stadiums will be surrounded by shops, housing, and popular tourist attractions.

Characteristics of 2030

- Cars will be replaced by flying machines, either person- or robot-powered (drones).
- Homes and businesses will be redesigned to use natural power more efficiently.
- All energy will come from wind, water power, and the efficient use of light.
- Oceans will provide drinking water.
- Life will extend to 100 to 120 years, with most people working until 80 to 90 years of age.

- People will plan for a number of careers and will continuously update employment skills to be competitive in the workforce.
- Extended life will be the result of genetic engineering and the replacement of body parts, particularly organs such as lungs. Diseases will have been eliminated.
- Agriculture will have moved from farmlands to urban highrise buildings.
- NASA technology will be commonplace and used by everyone.
- Money, as we know it, will no longer exist. New, global financial plans will guide people in saving and purchasing on the basis of lifestyles.
- All transportation will be by air. Roads and highways will become urban walking trails.
- No motorized vehicles will be used on these paths.
- Housing will continue to be individually owned but will favor group-oriented living before marriage and after child rearing. With changes in health and longevity, child rearing may last for a far longer period of time, with couples averaging 6 to 8 children.
- People will have moved inland from the coasts of oceans, rivers, and the Great Lakes; portable structures on water fronts will become prime vacation property.
- Planning for international sport will be massive.
- Camping, hiking, and so forth will be global.
- New sports will be invented.
- Events will be planned for all people, with the wealthier engaging in the most international travel.
- Sports will be club sports; intercollegiate and interscholastic sport will have disappeared.
- Space travel will be available for the masses.
- Space diving will be an important sport.

Characteristics of 2050

- Government and society will be global.
- Transportation, by air, will occur around the globe and to the moon and space platforms.
- Vehicles for short trips will be personally owned and will be launched from home or business; a number of different kinds of vehicles, yet to be designed, will be used for various types and lengths of travel.
- Sun, wind, and water will provide all necessary power.
- Living quarters will store energy from one season to the next. Oceans and winds will supply remaining needs.
- Persons will live to 120 to 130 years of age, working until 90 or 100 years of age. The change in longevity will be attributed to planned genetic sequences of individuals before birth, the eradication of diseases, and improved nutrition and emotional controls.
- Nutrition will change, with food, as we know it today, used only for festivals.
- Should urban farms succeed, food may remain as is. Urban farm failure may mean that people will eat nutritional pills instead of food.
- Sport events will be global, with levels of competition provided for both advanced and expert athletes, from youth to seniors.
- The global economy will enhance global travel for business and pleasure.

Preparing for the Future

Pink (2005) emphasizes the change that will occur with respect to right-brain people, who will become "creators and empathizers … meaning makers … and big picture thinkers" (p. 1). The Information Age rewarded the left brain, or rational, analytic, and logical minds. The Conceptual Age will reward nonlinear thinking, intuitiveness, empathy, and joy. Pink notes that the ability "to combine seemingly unrelated ideas into something new" will be highly rated (p. 2). More information about combing unrelated ideas can be found in DeBono's work on lateral thinking, a must-read in this area (DeBono, 1970). According to Pink (2005), the six senses are *design, story, symphony, empathy, play,* and *meaning.* Concerning *design,* he states that as a result of contemporary affluence, today's society wants products, services, and experiences to be beautiful or "emotionally engaging" (p. 65). Examples are the wide range of decorated cases available for cell phones and the decorated flip-flops found in our department stores. What was once a mere product for the beach has become a fashion statement. Furthermore, he believes that the ultimate form of persuasion and communication is the use of a *story* to make a point.

According to Pink (2005), *symphony* means synthesis, or seeing the big picture. It is this skill that will be most valued by sport specialists employed to design facilities and implement events. The planner who visions the finished product before placing the first word on paper has that "big picture" mind. *Empathy,* or the ability to walk in the shoes of another, is another of Pink's senses. Pink defines *empathy* as the "ability to understand what makes their fellow women tick, forge relationships, and to care for others" (p. 66). Sport marketing professionals need to examine *empathy* and place that quality high on their list of skills and attitudes. *Play,* a historical characteristic of the profession of sport, is another of Pink's six senses. *Laughter* and *humor* are among the characteristics he recommends that one acquire. Pink (2005), who often uses play, extends the concept to spontaneous nondirected goal activity. It is childlike movement and thinking. It is the freedom found in dance, gymnastics, and synchronized swimming. *Meaning,* what we do and what we provide for others, is the sixth, and last, of Pink's senses. By *meaning,* Pink (2005) means that vision which remains with us. For example, contrast your memories of walking through the gate at Daytona, sitting in the Super Bowl, yelling at the Orange Bowl, or freezing in the lounge after dark at the Salt Lake Olympics with similar television events. According to Pink, attending an event provides lasting memories seldom achieved by watching an event on electronic media. From all of Pink's work, the statement to take with you is: "Anyone can master the six Conceptual Age senses. But those who master them first will have a huge advantage" (Pink, 2005, p. 67). To be first to master these senses, or to find a niche, will be one of the most important achievements of the future.

Futurists tend to agree that in order to succeed or to plan for the future, one must change the way one thinks. Kida (2006), for example, cautions that we need to understand statistics, particularly probability theory, and use research rather than stories in making decisions. He notes that the ability to question an idea is more important than to merely confirm the idea. In addition, he suggests that we sometimes misperceive the world around us, oversimplify our thinking, and have faulty memories. In planning for the future, he recommends "strategic foresight." Gardner (2006), in *Five Minds for the Future*, presents the following: The *disciplined mind* has mastered one or more scholarly disciplines. Without at least one discipline, persons will be restricted to menial tasks. The *synthesizing mind* gathers information and research from a wide range of sources, analyzes the information objectively, and fashions the results into a coherent idea or statement. Without synthesizing skills, people will be overwhelmed by information. The *creative mind* generates new ideas, asks questions, and gains acceptance for the new ideas. Computers will replace all but the creative minds. The *respectful mind* appreciates and respects all forms of diversity and enjoys working with others. Those without appreciation and respect will harm the work environment. The *ethical mind* is empathetic to the needs and wishes of others. Those without ethics will harm the employer and coworkers (p. 18–19). He notes: "With these minds ... a person will be well equipped to deal with what is expected, as well as what cannot be anticipated; without these minds, a person will be at the mercy of forces that he or she can't understand, let alone control" (p. 2). Gardner (2006) makes the point that one cannot be creative in a subject until one knows the subject. In the following description of the creative emphasis in the United States in the 1980s, he states: "Everyone wanted to be creative; too many persons believed they were creative, even though they had scarcely begun to master a domain and even though no expert in the field would have judged them as creative.... Only through the honing of discipline would genuinely creative options ultimately emerge" (p. 85).

Naisbitt (2006) provides guidance in how to think. He mentions two important factors. First: "Understand how powerful it is not to have to be right" (p. xix). Doing so enables one to be creative—to retain a childlike approach to life. Second: "Don't get so far ahead of the parade that people don't know you're in it" (p. xix). In other words, work with others by using their familiar territory. He also recommends that when "looking for the shape of the future, look for and bet on the exploiters of opportunities, not the problem solvers" (p. 81). According to Lombardo (2006), future consciousness "improves higher-order thinking abilities ... expands mental and behavior freedom ... can work against depression, fear, apathy and perceived helplessness ... and brings greater self-control over one's life" (p. 49). Sport managers need to know that Gardner (2006) predicts: "Design and creativity are one of the key competitive advantages companies in developed economics can have—probably the only one they have left.... Fifteen years ago companies competed on price, now it's quality. Tomorrow it's design" (p. 124). Gardner (2006) goes on to quote Scott Morrison: "The aim today is to create products and services that 'look sharp, function intuitively, and wake some sort of positive emotional response from the consumer'" (p. 124). According to Canton (2006), if you want to be proactive rather than reactive you can influence your future by adopting the following:

1. A future vision—clear vision.
2. A sound strategy to get there.
3. Tools to persuade key people—colleagues, teammates, family members, and so on—to commit to a shared vision and strategy.
4. Effective execution.

To be ready for the future, Canton (2006) recommends the following future ready skills:

1. A positive outlook on the future.
2. Family and community involvement: a commitment to values.

3. Higher education.
4. Science and tech skills.
5. Financial awareness skills and personal money management.

Hines (2006) suggests six phases to be used in any order that seems appropriate to the leader or visionary. These phases will, hopefully, lead to clarity, creativity, and confidence. One phase is a comprehensive approach to problem identification and alternative scenarios. Here, objectives and outcomes are identified. Much of this phase is typical of existing planning systems; however, emphasis is placed on many alternatives rather than one path. Scanning, for example, in the organizational context, is the internal and external forces that fit an organization into the world in general. The remaining phases are as follows: 1) envisioning alternate futures; 2) identifying those preferred; 3) bridging the gap between the vision and action; 4) tailoring tactics and strategies to the organization; and 5) outlining the action phase, or how to carry out the vision (Hines, 2006). In addition to being a great planning process, the Hines system appears to engender employee loyalty. This method expands today's planning process to incorporate the culture of the business—to require all in the business to envision the future of the company and each individual's role in the company.

Conclusion

Hopefully, this chapter enabled you to dream and to think of how the future will affect your life. Prediction, as you will have noticed, becomes more difficult as the distance grows. The successful sport management professional in the year 2020 will be sensitive to people, welcome change, anticipate the needs of society, and be quick to bring new programs into reality. He or she will not only welcome and embrace change; he or she will also recognize the merits of timing—the timing of program delivery—as an element of the change process. Sport management professionals will have challenging and exciting careers if they have the following characteristics:

- They are sensitive to people and the world around them.
- They are eager to dream.

- They are diligent planners.
- They are able to make thing happen.

Chapter 17

Recommendations

JF & HA:

Herb and I have had a ball writing this book together. We'd like to leave you with some basic things that we feel can make a difference from the lessons that we have learned.

- Ensure that our programs provide the best education available, in a safe environment with caring teachers and administrators committed to student success.
- Revise the Elementary and Secondary Education Act (No Child Left Behind) to give it common sense application. If that cannot be done, then scrap it!
- Focus on student knowledge and achievement and less on standardized test scores.
- Recruit and train the best and brightest to be in our classrooms. Establish salaries that are conducive to attract the best possible teachers.
- Improve the learning environment for low-income children.
- Use technology as a tool to illustrate a point you are making but never to replace the essence of the lesson.
- Teach to Retain information, not "To-the-Test."
- Work with our teachers after they enter the profession and not just when they begin teaching.
- Have a goal to make a difference in the lives of your students.
- Have standards and hold students accountable with consequences.
- Experience the learning process together with students.

- Improve the work environment and you will retain more teachers.
- Extracurricular activities are crucial in the educational process because students involved in extracurricular activities have better attendance, fewer disciplinary problems, better grades and higher graduation rates.
- Administrators should involve teachers to provide input on educational matters.
- Appreciate the support staff and demonstrate to them that they play a vital role in the success of the school.
- Ensure that students achieve minimum competencies before they are promoted.
- Hold students accountable for attendance, behavior and effort.
- Constantly re-evaluate educational programs to ensure they remain relevant and productive for students.

References

Annie Clement:

Aburdene, P. (2005). *Megatrends 2010.* Charlottesville, VA: Hampton Roads.

Bright light, big savings. (2007, July). *Popular Science, 271* (1), 28.

Brown, A. (2006). The robotic economy, Brave new world or return to slavery? *The Futurist 40* (4), 50–55.

Canton, J. (2006). *The extreme future.* New York, NY: Penguin Group.

Clement, A., & Hartman, B. (1994). *The teaching of physical skill.* Dubuque, IA: Brown/Benchmark.

Crossman, W. (2004). Voice in, voice out. *The Futurist, 38* (6), 27–28.

Crossman, W. (2004). *Voice in, voice out (VIVO).* Oakland, CA: Regent Press.

Custer, K. J. (2007). From mice to men: Genetic doping in international sports. *Hastings Int'l & Comp. L. Rev. 30* (1), 181.

DeBono, E. (1970). *Lateral thinking: Creativity step by step.* New York: Harper & Row.

Despommier, D. (2007, July). The vertical farmer [Interview by A. Feldman]. *Popular Science, 271* (1), 45–46.

Environment. (2007). *The Futurist, 41* (2), 8.

Gardner, H. (2006). *Five minds for the future.* Boston, MA: Harvard Business School Press.

Hines, A. (2006). Strategic foresight: The state of the art. *The Futurist, 40* (5), 18–21.

Kida, T. (2006). *Don't believe everything you think: The 6 basic mistakes we make in thinking.* Amherst, NY: Prometheus.

Kuang, C. (2007, July). A giant leap for housing. *Wired, 15* (7), 76.

Kupetz, A. H. (2007). Our cashless future. *The Futurist, 41* (3), 36–40.

Lombardo, T. (2006). Thinking ahead: The value of future consciousness. *The Futurist, 40* (1), 45–50.

Naisbitt, J. (2006). *Mind set.* New York, NY: HarperCollins.

Parks, J., & Zanger, B. (Eds.). (1990). *Sports and fitness management, career strategies and professional content.* Champaign, IL: Human Kinetics.

Pink, D. H. (2005). *A whole new mind.* New York, NY: Penguin Group.

Sweeney, J. (2007). SportCast: 10 controversial issues confronting the sports industry. *The Futurist, 41* (1), 35–39.

Toffler, A. (1980). *The third wave.* New York, NY: Bantam Books.

Tomorrow in Brief. (2007). *The Futurist, 41* (2), 2.

Waldrop, M. M. (1992). *Complexity.* New York, NY: A Touchstone Book.

Weed, S. (2007, July). High dive. *Popular Science, 271* (1), 52–57, 97–98.

Zey, M. G. (2005a). *The ageless society.* Power point presentation (zeywfs05).

Zey, M. G. (2005b). The super longevity revolution. *The Futurist, 39* (6), 16–21.

Recommended Reading

DeBono, E. (1970). *Lateral thinking: Creativity step by step.* New York, NY: Harper & Row.

Sterling, B. (2007, July). Dispatches from the hyperlocal future. *Wired, 15* (7), 161–166.

HA:

Appenzeller, H. & G. Lewis. (2008). *Successful Sport Management.* Durham, NC: Carolina Academic Press.

Bassett, P. (2012). *National Association of Independent Schools.* Interview with Bruce Stewart about NAIS. (Bbruceb.stewart@gmail.com)

Bell, Gerald. (1973). *The Achievers.* Chapel Hill, NC: Preston-Hill, Inc.

Bennis, W. (1989). *Why Leaders Can't Lead.* San Francisco, CA: Jossey-Bass Publishers.

Bennis, W., & B. Namus. (1997). *Leaders: Strategies for Taking Charge.* New York, NY: HarperBusiness.

Berezow, A. & Campbell, H. (2012, June 4). Quit fretting: US doing ok in science education. *USA Today*, p. A9.

Billick, Brian & J. Peterson. (2001). *Competitive Leadership.* Orlando, FL: Delta Books.

Campbell, D. (1991). *Issues and Observations.* Greensboro, NC: Center for Creative Leadership.

Carr, N. (2011, September). New Missouri law shows the need for social media guidelines. *eSchool News*, 95–97.

Character 21, July 13, 2009.

Domenech, D. (2102, January). US education is still the best in the world—But here's what we can learn from others. *eSchool News*, pp. 99–101.

From the Gym to the Jury, *23* (2). (2011).

Fuller D., Sabiston, C., Karp, I., Barnett, T, & O'Loughlin, J. (2011). School sports opportunities influence physical activity in secondary school and beyond. *Journal of School Health*, *81*, 449–454.

Gormley, W. (2012, August 14). What our schools need? A few good men. *USA Today*, A7.

"Instructional rounds" flip classroom evaluations. (2011, July/August). *eSchool News*, 16.

Kleitman, S & Marsh, H. (2002). Extracurricular activities: The good, the bad, and the nonlinear. *Harvard Educational Review*, *72*, 464–515.

Lin, R. (2011, September). Study asks: What makes an effective school principal? *eSchool News*, 90–91.

Martin, L. & D. Mutchler. (2001). *Fail-Safe Leadership*. Orlando, FL: Delta Books.

Missouri teachers protest social media crackdown. (September 2011). *eSchool News*, 17–18.

Nearly 900 districts apply for Race to the Top grants. (2012 October). *eSchool News*, 82–83.

Placek, Christopher. (2012, September 27). 20 Glenbard S. athletes disciplined over Facebook photo. *Daily Herald*. Retrieved from: http://www.dailyherald.com/article/20120927/news/709279641/.

Pringle, Becky. (2012, August 8). Hold everyone accountable. *USA Today*, A6.

School reform news: Once-a-year teacher evaluations not enough. (2012, February). *eSchool News*, 104–105.

Stewart, Bruce. Interview. Sidwell Friends School, August 2012.

Study reveals teens' experiences on social media sites. (2012, January). *eSchool News*, 14–16.

Welsh, P. (2012, July 10). Why our kids hate math. *USA Today*, p. A7.

Index